Past-into-Present Series

MONEY

Alan James

B. T. BATSFORD LTD London

First published 1973
© Alan James 1973

Printed in Great Britain by
Redwood Press Limited, Trowbridge, Wiltshire
for the publishers
B. T. Batsford Ltd, 4 Fitzhardinge Street, London W1H 0AH

ISBN 0 7134 1787 0

Contents

Acknowledgment

The Author is grateful to the Deputy Master at the Royal Mint for details of modern coin presses, to the Secretary of the Bank Education Service for information provided to the Publicity Manager, Securicor Ltd, to the Press and Information Department o Barclays Bank Ltd, to Peter Cowey, a computer programmer, for information abou computers and to B. M. Wyllie, bank manager with Lloyds Bank for information abou mechanical devices.

The Author and Publisher would also like to thank the following for the illustrations Bank of England for figs 21, 31, 40; Barclays Bank for figs 26, 27, 28, 33, 37, 57, 58, 59 British Airports Authority for fig 34; the British Museum for figs 6, 8, 13; Camera Pres for fig 53; Chubb Ltd for fig 30; the *Daily Telegraph* for fig 56; Institute of Bankers c Scotland for fig 23; Johnson, Matthey and Co Ltd for fig 49; the Mansell Collectio for figs 2, 3, 9, 10, 11, 12, 14, 16, 17, 19, 20, 22, 24, 33, 45; Midland Bank for fig 35 National Bank of Detroit for fig 54; National Westminster Bank for figs 32, 36, 50, 52 55; Popperphoto for figs 18, 46; the Press Association for fig 51; the Post Office fo fig 61; Royal Bank of Scotland for fig 25; Securicor Ltd for figs 41, 42; the Science Museur (Crown copyright) for fig 7; Spinks Ltd for fig 18; Zurich Stock Exchange for fig 48.

The Illustrations

To Janet and Peter

1 The First Kinds of Money

Barter

In New York City the Chase Manhattan Bank has a Museum of Moneys of the World where there are more than 70,000 examples of things that have been used as money in different periods and in different places. In very early times, before men thought of using money, they had to exchange things directly and this often proved to be a difficult task. One man might have fish for sale and another might have pots. The two men might agree to swap—or barter—their possessions but all kinds of problems arose. How many fish were worth a pot? The two men would often have different ideas of the respective value of the two articles and argument and time-wasting would result. Suppose the fisherman had only a few fish for sale—worth only half a pot. Suppose the fisherman didn't want a pot but wanted fish-hooks instead. The pot-maker who wanted fish would have to find someone with fish-hooks for sale who wanted a pot. Then the trouble would start again; how many fish-hooks are worth a pot? Having got fish-hooks the pot-maker would take them to the fisherman and swap them for fish. But you can easily see how complicated the whole thing could become. If the man with fish-hooks had wanted spear heads instead of a pot—as could easily have been the case—the situation would have become ludicrous and men would have spent their time rushing round to find a seller with the right article who also happened to want the article they themselves had for sale.

Then in many places a different way of exchanging goods was devised. Oxen and cows were wanted by most people and almost everyone was prepared to accept them in exchange for things they had for sale. These animals became a kind of money. But animals used as money presented great problems. They died in the end. They could not be split up and still be used as money so they were useless for small transactions. But for larger exchanges they served a useful purpose and it is remarkable how widely they were used in this way. Words in use today remind us of the importance of cattle in trading in earlier times. The Indian coin called the rupee comes from the word *rupa* meaning a herd of cattle.

Goods as money

Many other commodities were used in the same way as cattle—as a standard value that was accepted by everyone in the community. This standard might be bronze axes as in Crete and Italy, bronze knives and metal rings in China, stone wheels on islands in the Pacific, fish in Alaska, cocoa beans in Mexico, rice in India, pieces of gold in Persia, beads in parts of Africa, butter in Norway, iron bars in France, tobacco in Virginia, salt in Nigeria and rats on Easter Island.

The list is almost endless. But once a certain article became accepted as money, trading problems were greatly simplified. Now the man with fish for sale merely had to sell it to anyone who wanted to buy it. In exchange he received 'money' in whatever form it was recognised in his locality, and with this money he could buy pots straight from the pot-maker without any of the previous fuss. Most of these early kinds of money—rice, tea, bricks, fish, salt, knives, fur, shells—were useful things in themselves; they were used in exchange but they could also be used in other ways too. Another value of these kinds of money was that most of them would last for a long time so that they could be kept until the right time to exchange occurred.

1 The Egyptians used barter for trading. They did not adopt coined money until about 300 BC. Here an Egyptian is weighing gold

Different though most of these items of money seem from our coins and bank-notes of today, they all had the same fundamental use. They could be kept for long periods. Many of them could be divided into small parts for minor transactions. They were recognised as money and used as a medium of exchange. Also they were used as a standard of value because people compared the commodities in terms of the amount of money each was worth. Of course, many of these kinds of money were far from perfect.

Money should be portable; heavy metal bars, elephant tusk and oxen do not fulfil this requirement easily. It should also be possible to divide money into smaller parts; a cow or a knife is not ideal from this viewpoint. Money should last for long periods; edible rats and butter have a limited life-span. Another important characteristic is that the article should be acceptable to everyone as money and that every such article should have the same value. Cowrie shells were commonly used as money in certain areas but if a man from a cowrie shell area wanted to trade with someone from a fish-hook area he might find that there was no way in which he could agree with the other trader. Fish-hooks were of no use as money in the cowrie shell area and *vice versa*. The two men might well turn to barter to exchange what they had for sale.

The money article must not be so common that it can be found easily. The saying 'money doesn't grow on trees' could be changed in this connection to 'money *shouldn't* grow on trees' for if it does, people can have as much money as they like simply by picking it up. Shells could not be used as a satisfactory money form if every day a tide brought a huge crop of new shells to the beaches. The money article must be restricted to make it of value. If it is commonly found then no-one will exchange their possessions for it.

Metal money

In time, the earlier forms of money were dispensed with and metals were used universally. They were not so heavy and cumbersome as some other money forms, they lasted for a lifetime, they could be divided into smaller parts fairly easily and they were not available in such plentiful supplies to make their value low. Gold and silver were the two metals that were used commonly. A certain weight in metal would be the price of an article and merchants weighed the metal on scales. In Genesis (Chapter 23) we read 'I will give thee money for the field . . . And Ephron answered him . . . the land is worth 400 shekels of silver . . . And Abraham weighed to Ephron the silver, which he had named in the audience of the sons of Heth, 400 shekels of silver, current money with the merchant'.

Great civilisations in the ancient world managed without the use of coins. No coins have been found in any of the Egyptian pyramids. The Babylonians, like the Egyptians, had metal weights made in exact sizes to use as standards in exchanges. Wall paintings from Egypt show pictures of precious metals being weighed against these standard weights—often gold rings, lambs and bronze calf-heads. Archaeologists digging at Ninevah, the ancient Assyrian city, found

2 This money box is of Roman
origin and was probably used as
a savings bank

evidence of similar standard weights in the shape of bronze lions and stone ducks.
Weights and scales formed part of the stock-in-trade of the merchant and the
wealthy but the poor people continued to barter in order to get hold of the
necessities of life.

Later, pieces of metal were cut up into exact weights and quality and stamped
to this effect; these were the first coins. Historians believe that the Chinese and
the Greeks both began to use coins at about the same time—700 BC. In Greece,
coins were first made in Lydia where gold was found mixed with silver in the
ground. The mixture was called *electrum* and the Lydians smelted it and made it
into small pieces of soft metal which were punched with an identifying mark.
Soon other Greek states and other countries began to make coins. Athens made
different values of silver coins in the fifth century BC. Pictures of eagles, owls,
dolphins and many other designs began to be used on coins, and later figures in
action and portraits were also incorporated in the designs.

Striking the coins

Each city state had its own mint and the coins of each city were identified by a certain emblem—Lydia had a lion and Aegina a turtle. Coins were improved in thickness and in shape as minters became more experienced in their work. Molten metal was made into small round blanks and the striker, in one careful movement, impressed the design on both sides of the coin. The design was impressed on an upper die (the trussell) and on a lower die (the pile). The blank coin was placed over the pile, and the trussell was levelled over the blank and given a sharp bang with a hammer weighing several pounds. Much experience was needed for the striker to make a good impression; too slight a tap would mean a poor impression on the coin but too hard a bang might split the die itself, and unless the trussell was held directly over the blank—without being tilted to either side—the impression would be a poor one with one part of the coin cut too heavily and the other part poorly impressed.

The first coins made by the Romans were rough bronze bars that did not have a value or a standard weight marked on them. They differed from the Greek coins in being cast from moulds and were not struck from dies. Later Roman coins were struck from coin dies in the same way that Greek coins were made. The Romans manufactured coins on a more businesslike basis than the Greeks for they needed vast numbers of coins for their many territories, and a single system of coinage helped to unify such territories into a composite whole. The Roman coin-strikers placed the lower die in a hollow on the anvil which allowed a more accurate impression in the centre of the blank. The Romans also

3 The payment of taxes is shown on this Roman funeral stone of the third century AD

invented a hinged die—rather like a pair of tongs—but its use was limited as a badly-aimed strike could easily damage the die.

The Roman mint was established in the temple of the goddess Juno who was given the title 'Moneta' from which comes our word 'money'.

Further reading
R. Nitsche, *Money* (Collins)
A. H. Quiggin, *Story of Money* (Methuen)

2 Early Coinage in Britain

Roman coins in Britain

In 1879 a votive accumulation of about 16,000 Roman coins, mainly bronze, was discovered at Carrawburgh near Hadrian's Wall on the site of the well of the water nymph Coventina. In addition were found many brooches and pins, all of which were thrown into the well as offerings to the goddess.

Finds of coin hoards occur in the most unlikely places and sometimes add

4 Coins used in Roman Britain from the end of the third to the fifth centuries AD:
1 Carausius
2 Allectus
3 Constantine the Great
4 Maximian
5 Constantine III
6 Magnus Maximus

greatly to the store of historical knowledge for any area. A hoard of more than 1,200 gold coins from medieval times was found at Fishpool in Nottinghamshire in 1966 which was the largest find of medieval gold coins ever discovered and which included a quarter-noble of Edward IV's reign—a previously unknown coin.

Coin finds must be reported to the authorities—stealing by finding is a punishable offence—and a coroner then decides on the ownership of the hoard. If it is decided that the coins are Treasure Trove they belong to the Crown, though compensation is given to the finder. Treasure Trove is gold and silver (not copper or bronze coinage) which the original owner buried and which he intended to reclaim at a later date but was unable to do—perhaps because of death or war. The coroner may decide that a find is not Treasure Trove if it had been buried permanently and there was no intention to dig it up again later, and then the treasure belongs to the owner of the land on which it was found. This was the case with the priceless finds from the Sutton Hoo Treasure Ship but the owner presented the treasure to the nation and it can be seen today in the British Museum.

Iron rings and iron bars are mentioned by Caesar. Iron bars shaped like sword blades have been discovered by archaeologists on British sites dated to the first century BC. In the same century gold coins were used in Britain, probably minted in Gaul (now France). Tin money was made and used in Britain, the

5 These bronze Roman money balances were used in the middle of the fourth century AD. There are two sets of weights, ranging from the half-solidus to 36-solidi. The balances and the weights fitted inside the wooden case and tray

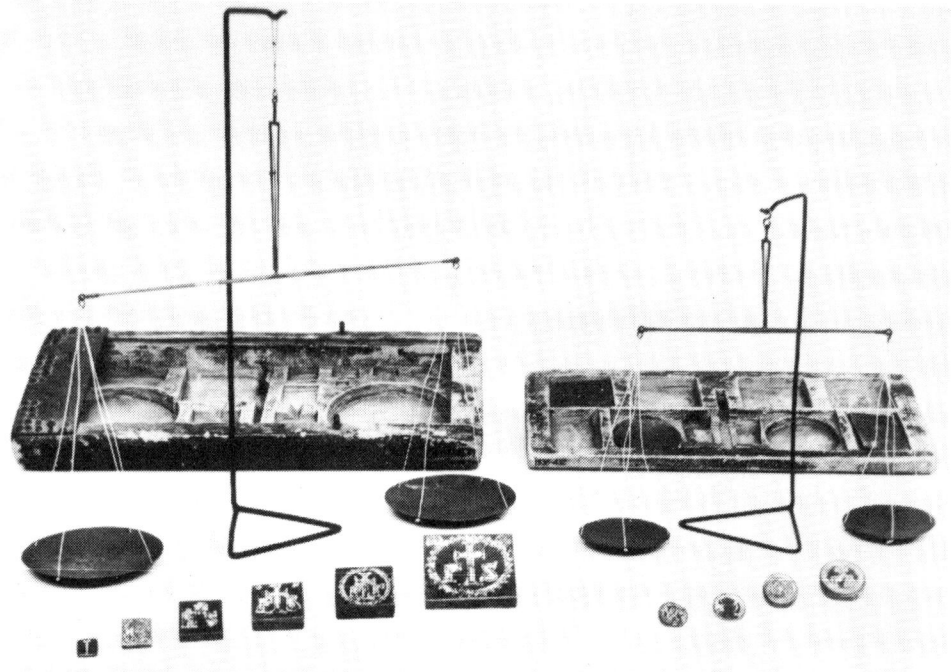

coins being cast in strips. Papyrus coin shapes were pressed into clay moulds. Soon after, gold coins were struck in Kent. Though some coins continued to be cast in moulds—such as the bronze coins of the Durotriges in the West Country—most ,of the gold, silver and bronze coins used in Iron Age Britain were struck between dies. Many of the chiefs and tribal kings of Britain issued their own coins which makes the study of numismatic history in this period very complex.

There were only official mints in Roman Britain during certain periods in the latter half of the Roman occupation. Coins were supplied from the mint at Rome and from the Imperial Mint at Lugdunum (Lyons). During the first part of the Roman occupation, pre-conquest coinage served alongside the Roman gold, silver and bronze coins—silver being the most important metal. One British mint was sited at London and the moneyers were skilled workers who made coins of high quality. Roman coins are of particular historical interest as they show portraits of emperors and sometimes commemorate victories and important events. The Roman word for an amount of silver weighing one pound—*libra*—has been preserved in our £ sign.

The Anglo-Saxons

The Roman forces left Britain in the year AD 410 and much coinage went with them. Many people remaining in Britain must have reverted to barter. The renewed prosperity which occurred during the Anglo-Saxon period resulted in a fresh impetus to coining. A mint was established at Canterbury to make gold coins. These were later replaced by silver. During the late eighth century, silver pennies were minted and this silver denomination remained in use for over five hundred years. For purchases of a lower value than one penny, the coin had to be cut in half or quartered. The coins were not always divided accurately and extra pieces were sometimes clipped off, collected and then melted into valuable pieces of silver. By the start of the tenth century the Vikings struck pennies and half-pennies in London.

During Aethelstan's reign, in the first half of the tenth century, there were nearly thirty mints throughout the country. Transporting money from one central mint was difficult and dangerous and a multiplicity of mints speeded coin pro-duction and reduced the risks of serious robbery. Aethelstan proclaimed that the loss of a hand should be the punishment for forgery. A fixed number of moneyers was allowed at each mint. The mint at Canterbury was allowed seven moneyers, London was allowed eight, other mints had two and the small mints had only one. In the reign of Edward the Confessor, ending in 1066, there were about seventy mints. The central mint was sited in London and as each mint paid fees to the central one the king obtained a valuable source of revenue by this means. The Norman Conquest changed coinage very little. The silver penny was kept in circulation.

Early Anglo-Saxon coin dies had been engraved by hand. By the ninth century the design was cut by using punches—rather like tiny chisels. Molten metal from which coins were to be made was poured out, allowed to cool and then hammered to the required thickness. It was then cut into round blanks. Each blank was positioned over the lower die which was pointed at one end and secured firmly into a large piece of wood to hold it steady. The upper die was heavier because it was hit with the hammer. In fact, several upper dies were needed during the time one lower die took to wear out. A set of dies could make thousands of coins. The name of the moneyer at each mint was struck as part of the design of the coin. The moneyer could be called to account if the coins did not conform to required weights and qualities of metal and impression.

Medieval coins

By the end of the twelfth century there were only eleven mints. Kings were finding it much easier to control a few large mints than many small ones. In 1247 Henry III's Long Cross coins were brought into circulation in place of the

6 A medieval banker weighing coins. Interest rates were high in the middle ages because all interest—and not just excessive interest—was regarded as the 'damnable sin' of usury. The highest legal rate of interest was fixed at 10 per cent in the sixteenth century, and at 5 per cent in the eighteenth century. The Usury Laws were repealed totally in 1854

7 A sixteenth-century mint from a woodcut by Hans Burgkmair. The metal is melted in a furnace, the metal plate is being beaten (centre), coin blanks are cut out (left) and the striker is shown at work (right). Coins are being weighed in the background. Some coins were placed in a chest for assay checks on the quality of production

Short Cross issues. The Long Cross on each coin prevented people from clipping off part of the coin dishonestly because if they attempted to do so then part of the cross disappeared and this was apparent at a glance. Coins had to be of the exact weight and moneyers were in serious trouble if they minted coins below the required weight: 20 pennies weighed one ounce, and 240 pennies weighed the same as a pound of silver.

In 1280 Edward I ended the practice of cutting up coins to obtain pieces of metal for small transactions. He issued groats—fourpence pieces—pence, halfpence and farthings. These coins were so well-designed that it was many years before their influence ceased to affect later issues and also coins issued abroad. In the mid-fourteenth century Edward III issued the noble which was a gold coin showing the king in a sailing boat holding weapons. There were also half- and quarter-nobles to cater for the wider needs of the population as trade and commerce grew in importance.

The Tudors

In 1489 Henry VII minted the first gold sovereign—which was at that time the largest English coin ever produced. His son, Henry VIII, like other kings before him, reduced the amount of valuable metal in each coin. Henry VIII debased the gold as well as the silver coinage on several occasions during his reign. In an age when the metal content of gold or silver in coins was still regarded as important, debasement was a risky process. The value of the metal in a coin was at that time regarded as equal to the face value stamped on it. These are called standard coins. But Henry VIII reduced the valuable metal content of coins so greatly— substituting base metal—that coins had only about one-seventh of the silver that the coins at the beginning of his reign had contained. The rise in the value of precious metals and the practice of debasing the amount of valuable metal in a coin resulted in a gradual movement away from standard coins and an acceptance over the centuries of token coins—coins made of metal that is of very little value compared with the face value.

In the following reign, Edward VI made gold coins of 22-carat in place of the previous 20-carat coins. Silver shillings were made in different sizes but there were also base silver coins. So many coins were in circulation, each with its own metal value, that the public must have had difficulties in attempting to interpret the respective values of coins of the same denomination, and sharp practices resulted.

Elizabeth I had many coins struck including sovereigns, ryals, angels, pounds and crowns. Some of these coins were also struck in half and quarter values. The humbler silver coins included shillings, sixpences, groats, three half-pennies, pence and half-pence.

Tokens and copper coins

In the 1570s there was a shortage of coins of low value and shopkeepers used lead and tin token coins during this period to overcome the deficiency. This was, however, an illegal measure though in 1577 Bristol obtained a licence to strike square farthings made of copper. The use of token coins grew over the next hundred years and many forged token farthings were made. Many towns also had token half-pence. James I and Charles I issued royal licences for the making

8 (*opposite*) 1 copper penny, George III; 2 copper half-penny, Charles II; 3 base testoon, Henry VIII; 4 silver florin, Edward VII; 5 bronze coin, Constantine the Great; 6 silver shilling, George II; 7 copper half-farthing, Victoria; 8 silver fourpence piece, William IV; 9 first round silver half-penny, Alfred (?); 10 first silver penny, Ecgberht

of copper farthing tokens. In 1672 Charles II minted copper coinage for the country and so the use of tokens declined. At first blank copper discs were bought from Sweden and the stamping was done in England. Later, tin was used instead, though it corroded in time.

For hundreds of years until the seventeenth century the gold and silver bars from which coins were made were cut into small pieces of a certain weight and then were stamped with a design by a blow from a hammer which struck the design on the coin. This method was slow and laborious and unsuited to the needs of a nation demanding ever-increasing supplies of coin. Methods of hammering coins had changed little since early times. The pictures of mints in this chapter show the moneyer and his assistants at work and it can be seen that the basic tools of the trade were few and simple. Mints were not imposing centres of manufacture; they were rather like untidy little workshops. Mints were sometimes moved from town to town as the king directed. It can be seen from contemporary pictures that it would be an easy job to make the necessary implements to counterfeit coins. Dishonest workers at official mints could easily stay late at night and make coins for their own use or remove dies to a hidden workshop for the night. Punishment for counterfeiting was harsh and included such extremes as mutilation, hanging, blinding and burning.

Machinery for mints

The use of machinery in striking coins meant that far more coins could be produced than ever before. Machinery was used in the mint at Paris in the mid-sixteenth century and it was introduced into London for a short period during the reign of Elizabeth I. The screw press was powered by human muscle or by horses. Each press needed three men to work it, and could produce about twenty-five coins a minute. It was not so easy to clip these coins as it had been with the old hammered ones. But the hammering of coins did not stop entirely until 1662.

Thick bars of metal were put through the rolling press and this changed them into thin sheets from which coin blanks—all of the same weight—could easily be cut. The screw press squeezed the design on the coin blank. Two men swung the arms on the earliest type of screw press and this raised and lowered the die. A third man put a coin blank into the press between the dies and then took it out when the design had been struck on it. The coin setter had to be careful that his fingers were not crushed and he had to keep his head low or the powerful arms on the press would knock him over.

In the eighteenth century steam was used by Matthew Boulton and James Watt to power coining machines; and later still electrical power was used instead.

Further reading
T. W. Becker, *The Coin Makers* (Doubleday)
G. Berry, *Discovering Coins* (Shire Publications)

3 Modern British Coins

The astronomer Isaac Newton was Master of the Mint in the first part of the eighteenth century. One of the greatest problems towards the end of the seventeenth century had been the constant clipping, filing and debasing of the coinage. The country had a bimetallic money system and both the gold and the silver coins in circulation were subject to constant abuse. In 1695, for instance, the silver coins were so badly clipped that a complete silver recoinage became necessary.

Coins in short supply

The economic system throughout Britain changed in focus and intensity in the eighteenth century, but an adequate supply of coins to meet this increased trading and commercial situation was not forthcoming. The previous chapter showed something of the problems created by a multiplicity of coins of different metal content and how difficult it must have been to assess their respective values. To make matters worse, English and Scottish coins were valued at different levels until the union in 1707. The English silver shilling circulated in Ireland at a value of one shilling one penny. England would have been even more badly-placed in the number of coins in circulation at this time if she had not stolen coins from Spain. Several treasure ships were taken in Vigo Bay and more than eleven million silver pieces of eight were transported to England. Some gold was also taken and, along with the silver, was made into English 'Vigo' coins. The seizing of this Spanish treasure helped to ease the shortage of coins in the early part of the eighteenth century, but coins of low denominations were desperately needed, though farthings were issued in the latter part of the seventeenth century.

The reader is referred at the end of this chapter to other books which tell in detail the story of British coins, reign by reign. In the next few pages a very brief review will be given of some of the main coining developments over the last three hundred years.

George I (1714–1727) minted a gold quarter-guinea in addition to the usual gold guinea denomination and the silver coins included crowns, half-crowns, shillings, sixpences, fourpences, twopences and pence. There were copper halfpence, and also farthings nicknamed dumps because they were small and fat.

George II (1727–1760) minted five, two, one and also half-guineas in gold. Silver coins were struck in a variety of denominations and both these and most of the gold coins were made from treasure taken from yet another raid on a Spanish ship and from raids by Anson on Lima in Peru. Copper coins were also struck but from the middle of the century silver and copper coins became difficult to find in quantity. Supplies of metal became scarce. The government had not

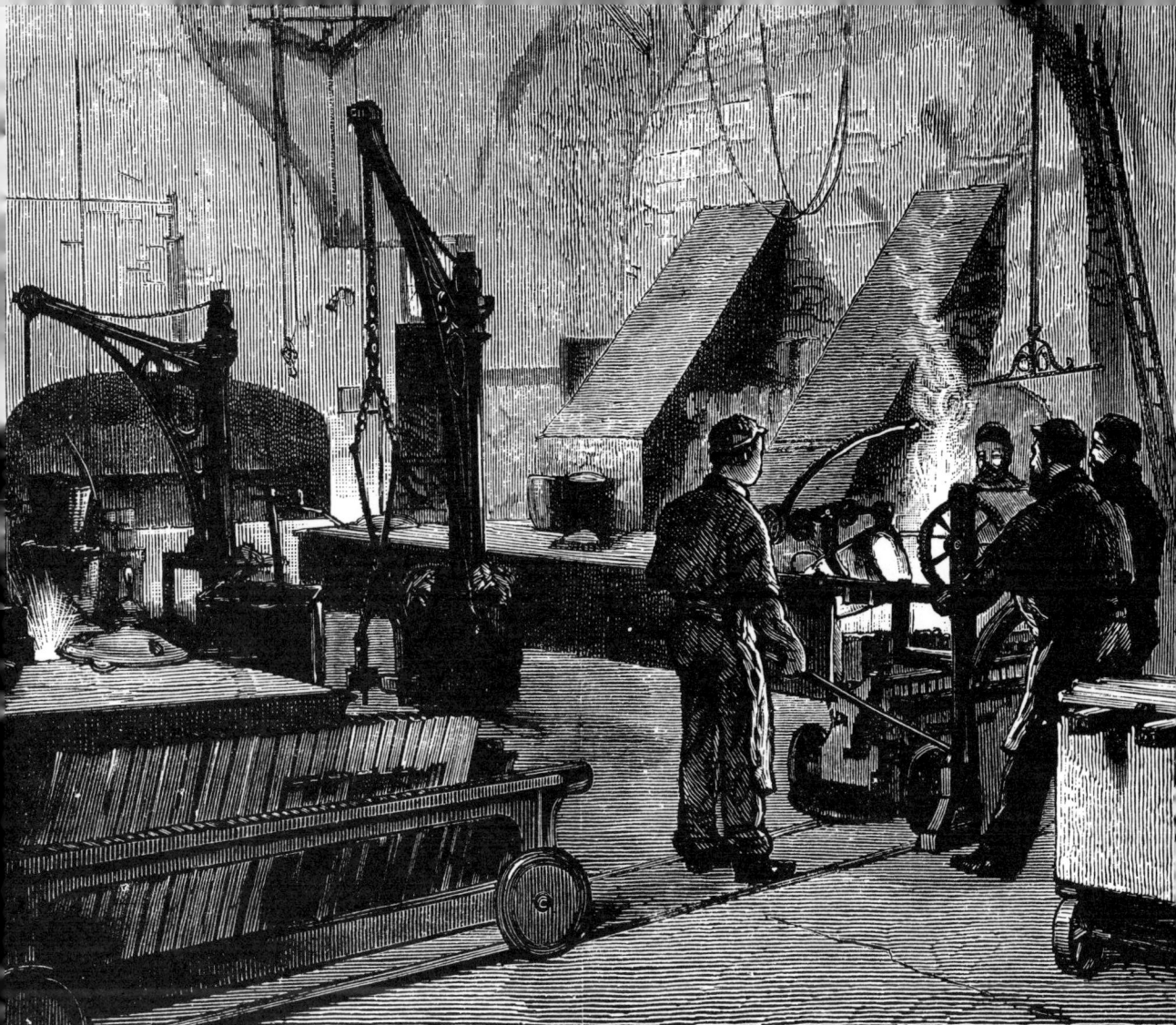

10 The silver melting room at the Royal Mint, 1883

been greatly worried about the counterfeiting of copper coins but from 1742 culprits could be sentenced to prison for two years. However, token copper coins were allowed if there was no intention to deceive people into believing that these were genuine coins. In a book published in 1751 it is recorded 'There are now almost infinite sorts. Every town and village has its mints where many of our master manufacturers get them coined as cheap as they can for their own use to pay their workmen with'. Some contemporaries estimated that there might even have been more token copper coins in circulation than legal ones!

In the reign of George III (1760–1820) it was found necessary virtually to replace gold coin with banknotes. Hardly any silver or copper coins were minted

11 One of the rolling rooms at the Royal Mint, 1883. Metal is rolled into strips of the required thickness before being stamped out as coin blanks

either. The Welsh and West of England mines had become worked out. After 1758 few silver coins were made for about thirty years. For nearly twenty years from 1754 there were no new copper coins. Later in the reign there were various issues of copper coins which were very badly needed for all kinds of minor transactions. Tokens, now illegal despite their great usefulness, continued to be circulated. Silver dollars from various countries were stamped with George III's head in 1797 and were circulated in Britain as legal coins. These coins were withdrawn before the end of George III's reign. Naturally they were objects of fun:

> The Bank of England, to make their dollars pass,
> Stamped the head of a fool on the head of an ass.

This measure, strange though it might appear, merely made legal an existing state of affairs, for dollars had already been circulating in Britain unofficially.

Silver becomes a token coinage

In 1816 silver became a token coinage—because currency was put on a gold standard—and the weight of new silver coins was reduced. In that year old silver was called in and new silver coinage was minted. The values were the half-crown, the shilling and the sixpence. Prior to the decimal changeover in 1971, British silver coins going back to 1816 were all regarded as legal tender, though seldom were coins earlier than Victorian ones passed from hand to hand. In the same way, bronze coins dating from 1860 were all legal tender.

George IV (1820–1830) issued gold two-pound coins and sovereigns, as well as silver coins. Farthings, half-pence and pence were issued in copper.

His successor, William IV (1830–1837), had a short-lived reign and full sets of all denominations were not issued. There were gold sovereigns and half-sovereigns. Fourpenny silver coins—called groats—were minted again and these coins showed Britannia on the reverse. Groats were something of an innovation for they had not been used since the seventeenth century. Copper coins were issued in the familiar low values as well as half- and third-farthings which were minted for use in Ceylon and Malta respectively.

During the reign of Queen Victoria (1837–1901) there were various issues of coins. The first are known as the 'Young Head' coins, the florins being issued as a trial in 1849 as a first step towards a system of decimal coinage. Other Victorian

12 Transporting money was dangerous as travellers might be attacked by highwaymen. The robbing of passengers virtually ceased when mail and passengers began to be carried by mail coaches. John Palmer started the service in 1784. Each mail coach carried an armed guard and many passengers favoured this as a safer vehicle than the stage coach. Between 1784 and 1792 not a single mail coach was stopped or robbed

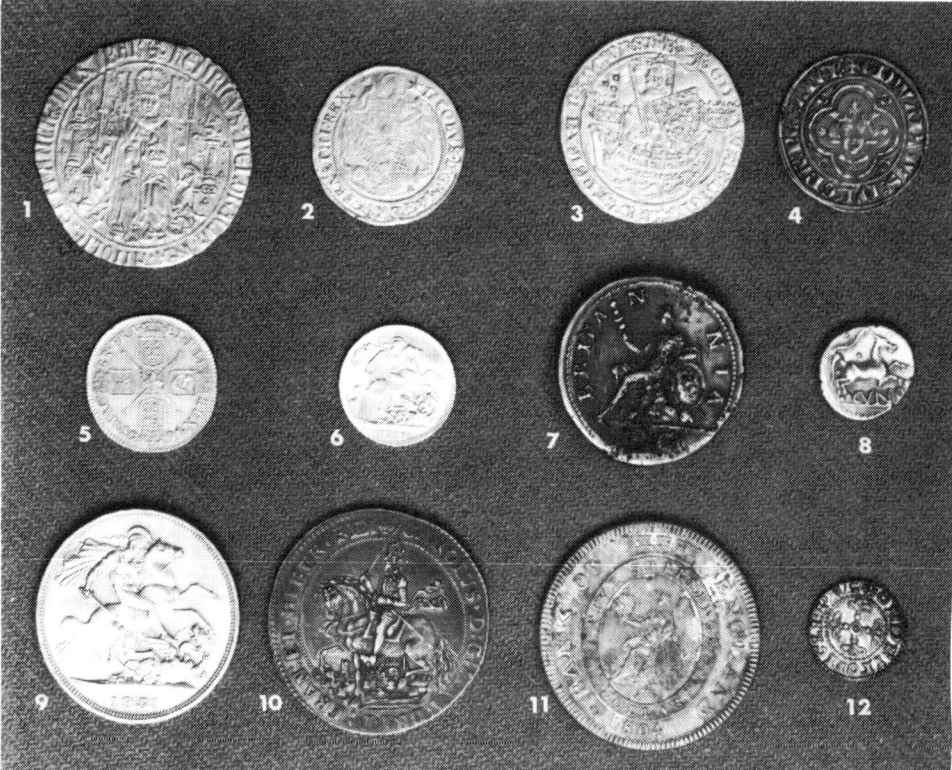

13 (opposite) 1 gold sovereign, Henry VII; 2 gold angel, James I; 3 gold noble, Edward III; 4 first silver groat, Edward I; 5 gold guinea, Charles II; 6 gold sovereign, George V; 7 brass sestertius, Antoninus Pius; 8 gold stater, Cunobeline; 9 silver crown, George VI; 10 silver Oxford, Charles I; 11 silver dollar, George III; 12 silver penny, William I

coins included sovereigns, half-sovereigns, half-crowns, shillings, sixpences, groats and threepences. Half-farthings were struck in bronze:

> Too small for any marketable shift,
> What purpose can there be for coins like these?
> Hush, hush, good Sir!—Thus charitable Thrift
> May give a mite to him who wants a cheese!

Bronze coins, made from a copper alloy of 95 per cent copper, 4 per cent tin and 1 per cent zinc, were struck from 1860 in place of the old copper coins.

The second issue of coins is known as the 'Jubilee' issue and dates from 1887. Unusual coins in this group included the five-pound and the two-pound coins in gold as well as double-florins—the four-shilling coins.

From 1893 the third and final coinage was minted and this is termed the 'Old Head' issue.

Victoria's son, Edward VII, reigned from 1901–1910 and the denominations of his coins were almost the same as those of his mother's long reign.

The first silver coins of George V (1910–1936) contained 92.5 per cent silver. From 1920 silver coinage only contained 50 per cent silver. The production of these new silver coins presented minting problems. At first, the mixture was 50 per cent silver, 40 per cent copper and 10 per cent nickel, but these coins soon became discoloured and unattractive. Experiments resulted in a new mixture— 50 per cent copper and no nickel—and this improved the appearance of the finished coins. Later, a further mixture was introduced—50 per cent silver, 40 per cent copper, 5 per cent nickel and 5 per cent zinc. The denominations of coins in the reign of George V remained much the same as previously. In 1933 only six pennies were minted.

New shapes, new designs

Edward VIII reigned for only a few months in 1936 before his abdication in December. No coins bearing the portrait of the new king went into circulation, since the king was never crowned, though the Mint was hard at work striking coins for the new reign; these were, of course, melted down. One new coin of this reign was the nickel-brass twelve-sided threepence which was to have replaced the small silver threepence coin. Most were melted down but a few of these twelve-sided coins survived and are extremely valuable; they are dated 1937.

George VI (1936–1952) saw the introduction of the new nickel-brass twelve-sided threepence coins. Another change was that the reverse of the other bronze

27

14 The screw press was used to make British coins from 1662 until the reign of George III. Two men swung the arms back and forward which raised and lowered the die head. A third operator pushed away the stamped coin and put a blank in its place. Between twenty and thirty coins could be struck in a minute

coins no longer bore the same design as the reverse of the pennies. Britannia was still used for the reverse of the pennies with a lighthouse as part of the design. The reverse of the half-penny showed a sailing ship and the reverse of the farthing a wren.

Silver disappears from coinage

It will be remembered that in 1920 the silver content in silver coins was reduced to 50 per cent. In 1947 British 'silver' coins ceased to contain any silver at all. Instead they were made of cupro-nickel—75 per cent copper and 25 per cent nickel. Pre-1920 and pre-1947 silver coins can still be discovered and these are worth more to the numismatist than cupro-nickel coins of later dates. But the banks and the Mint work together to replace these old coins with new ones. Banks remove worn and defaced coins from circulation and these coins—together with some other mixed silver coins which the banks return regularly to the Royal Mint—are fed into an electronic sorting machine which separates the real silver coins from the cupro-nickel ones. The latter are put into circulation again but the coins with a silver content are withdrawn and melted down. Very soon, all pre-1947 silver coins will be withdrawn from circulation.

Coin collectors who study the lettering round each coin will notice a change during the reign of George VI. In 1947 India and Pakistan changed their status in the British Empire and the lettering on coins 'Ind Imp'—which meant 'Emperor of India'—had to be removed. New coins were issued from 1949 without this title.

Commemorative crowns

The 1951 crown (worth 25p) with St George and the dragon on the reverse was so popular throughout the world that more than two million were minted— and sold mostly as souvenirs of the Festival of Britain.

The reign of Queen Elizabeth II began in 1952 and it is with the coins of this reign that many new coin collectors begin, and then start to work backwards. The obverse of the Coronation crown piece shows the Queen on horseback; a monarch on horseback had not appeared on our coins since the time of Charles I. The 1965 Winston Churchill commemorative crown is a unique issue which has the head of a commoner on one side and the head of the monarch on the other.

The decimal changeover

Farthings were withdrawn from circulation from the first day of 1961, and the old half-penny, the old penny, the threepence and the half-crown disappeared in the decimalisation changeover.

Earlier in this chapter it was noted that the florin was introduced in 1849 as an experimental coin—the first of Britain's decimal coins. But the idea of decimal coinage was far older than that. China had used a decimal-based currency since the eighth century; the United States of America established decimal coinage in the 1790s. France went decimal in 1783; further back still, Simon Stevin, a Dutch-man, wrote in 1586 about the inevitable introduction of decimal coins, as well as decimal weights and measures. In 1682 William Petty wanted to have five farthings to every penny to 'keep all accompts in a way of Decimal Arithmetik'; Christopher Wren wanted an ounce of silver to be sub-divided into hundredths; John Herschel was Master of the Mint in the mid-nineteenth century and he wanted to bring decimal coins to Britain, but the florin, as one-tenth of a pound, was the only coin he was able to introduce.

In 1951 a Board of Trade report spoke favourably about decimal coinage. By 1960 the British Association for the Advancement of Science and the Associa-tion of the British Chambers of Commerce were in favour of change. The Halsbury Committee in 1963 began to examine the practical possibilities of different kinds of decimal systems. Finally, decimal day came on 15 February 1971. The change-over was not so problematic as many people had feared. The pound note was left untouched and the cupro-nickel 10p and 5p coins (as the old florin and shilling) had been in use before the changeover. The new coins were the bronze ½p, 1p and 2p and the cupro-nickel 50p coin (which replaced the ten-shilling note) and which is the only seven-sided coin in the world. This coin should last for fifty

15 (*above and opposite*) Maundy Money is presented annually by the sovereign to a certain number of elderly people. The ceremony goes back for many centuries. 1 Victoria; 2 George III; 3 James II; 4 Elizabeth II

years or more, whereas the ten-shilling note needed to be destroyed after only a few months.

About 95 per cent of the world now uses decimal currency and Britain's change-over was becoming inevitable to fit more easily into the international monetary scene.

1   2

3   4

Maundy Money

Maundy Money is distributed annually by the sovereign to a certain number of deserving elderly people on Maundy Thursday—the Thursday before Easter Sunday. The ceremony originally was a re-enactment of the washing of the disciples' feet by Christ. St Augustine landed in Kent in the year 597 and the ceremony is at least as old as that. References occur sporadically through the pages of history. King John, in the early thirteenth century, gave money to the poor. In the sixteenth century Queen Mary 'gave to each a leathern purse containing forty-one pennies, according to the number of her years.'

The washing of the feet ritual ceased in the eighteenth century. The Maundy Money coins are now the only silver coins made in Britain and consist of 92.5 per

16 Coins were given to the sick by the king in the belief that the monarch had the power to heal. Charles II is said to have presented these touchpieces to 90,000 people. Touchpieces could be hung round the neck and the official on the left of the king is holding one of the coins. The practice seems to have died out in the early eighteenth century

cent pure silver. Usually the monarch distributes these coins—which are valuable both as metal and as collectors' pieces—at an annual service in Westminster Abbey or at one of the cathedrals throughout the country. Silver coins of one, two, three and fourpence are minted for this service and a number of men and women are selected (the number of those selected is the same as the sovereign's age) to receive them. Each person receives Maundy Money in an amount equivalent in pence to the age of the monarch. The coins are presented by the sovereign in a white purse.

The development of coining machines
Coining today is a very different matter from the situation of even two hundred years ago. Coins are now minted in such large numbers and by using such

sophisticated methods that it seems a long jump indeed back even to the first types of machine-made coins. In 1966 the Royal Mint in London made 1,400,000,000 coins. A modern mint probably produces more coins in a week than used to be made in a century. Before we conclude this chapter by looking at the work of the Royal Mint today, it is necessary first to find out how machines that make coins have developed into the complicated and automated machines which make our coins today.

In the latter part of the eighteenth century James Watt and Matthew Boulton used steam power to operate coining machines. At their Soho engineering works close to Birmingham a coin manufacturing complex was set up to provide coins for various countries, including Russia. In 1797 the plant began to make copper coins for Britain. Within two years it produced more than a thousand tons of copper coins. These coins were so well-made and standardised that forgery became a very difficult art to master. The coin blanks were stacked into a tube on the machine and then the machine took over the whole stamping process. Another machine even engraved the punches from which the dies were eventually made. The artist's model for the design of a coin was made in plaster. This was copied as a copper electrotype and was then fixed on the reducing machine. The reducing machine copied straight on the die a much smaller design from the large original one. A trace moved over the design and a cutting print engraved a reduced copy of the original design.

The Royal Mint

A mint had existed in London more or less continuously from Roman times. From the year 1300 the Mint was sited within the walls of the Tower of London. By the early nineteenth century the premises were becoming cramped for the volume of work that was done. A new building was sited on Tower Hill and this was completed in 1811. Boulton and Watt's steam-driven machinery, which

17 The Royal Mint's coining presses, 1883

operated the screw presses, was set up in this new building. The reducing machine was used by the Mint from 1824, and electric-powered machinery was used from 1905. In the latter part of the nineteenth century further building extensions occurred and more new machinery was introduced. The Mint was further extended in the twentieth century as the demand for United Kingdom, Commonwealth and foreign coins continued to increase rapidly. Output was increased by the staff working double shifts as well as night shifts.

Inevitably, however, the London Mint became too small to cope, especially with the production of the huge numbers of decimal coins which were required for the change to decimal money. The new Royal Mint at Llantrisant in Glamorgan, South Wales, was opened by the Queen in 1968. More than 4,000,000,000 new coins were needed for the decimal changeover. These were all manufactured at Llantrisant.

The Chancellor of the Exchequer was titled Master of the Mint under the 1870 Coinage Act; but the executive head is the Deputy Master and this office is held by a permanent civil servant. The work of the Mint is manifold. In addition to coins for the United Kingdom, some Commonwealth and some foreign countries, the Royal Mint manufactures medals and seals for the British and Commonwealth Governments, as well as making engraved plates for postage and revenue stamps. Medals and seals are even struck for the requirements of private customers.

Modern minting processes

Even a casual perusal of early coins compared with those of today reveals that coins have changed greatly in appearance and quality over the centuries. Some would argue that the creativity once so necessary in minting has now disappeared in favour of machine-made, standardised coins. Yet the perfection of mechanical processes—resulting in better shape, design and roundness—brings its own technical problems which need to be solved if modern coins are to be produced well. In ages gone by, the coin blank was struck by a hammer with a force of only a few pounds. Now the coin press thunders against the blank with tons of force. The engraving must be perfect, of course, for a poor engraving—however slight the imperfection—would become magnified on the actual coin.

The raw materials for coins are copper, nickel, tin and zinc. Copper ingots weighing about half a hundredweight come mainly from South Africa, Canada and Zambia. These are cut in half before entering the furnaces. Nickel comes from Canada in five-hundredweight drums but it is changed into pellets in Wales. Tin ingots come from Cornwall and plates of zinc come from Poland, Bulgaria and other countries in eastern Europe. Silver bars, used to make medals, come from North and South America, Russia and South Africa.

Cupro-nickel coins (5p, 10p and 50p) consist of 75 per cent copper and 25 per cent nickel. Bronze coins ($\frac{1}{2}$p, 1p and 2p) are made of 97 per cent copper, $\frac{1}{2}$ per cent tin and $2\frac{1}{2}$ per cent zinc.

18 A coiner at work in the Royal Mint. Most presses are fully automatic but coiners sometimes stamp out special coins to preserve their skills. This press can strike coins at the rate of 120 a minute

The main processes in the making of coins are as follows:

1 *Melting.* Cupro-nickel and bronze each melt in about 70 minutes. The melting takes place in electric or oil furnaces each of which holds about 850 lbs [380 kg] of metal. Molten metal is poured from electric furnaces at 1380°C and at two hundred degrees lower from oil furnaces. It is poured into moulds and the cast bars are cooled under water. Each bar is marked with letters of identification.

2 *Rolling.* The metal bars pass through heavy rolling mills about eleven times to break down the thickness. This stretches the bars which are then cut into more manageable lengths. The metal is later rolled to the thickness of coins. It may take a total of eighteen rollings before the bar is reduced to the right thickness.

3 *Cutting.* From two to six blanks are punched out on the cutting machine at every blow. These blanks are always slightly larger than the size of the ultimate coin. The scrap metal left over when the blanks have been punched is sent to be melted again and re-used.

4 *Annealing and Blanching*. During the rolling the metal hardens. In order that it can be stamped it has to be softened, and the process is known as annealing. The blanks are passed through gas-fired furnaces at temperatures reaching 700°C. They appear as red-hot discs that are covered in oxide. These are cooled by being plunged into water and are then put into blanching barrels where the oxide is removed from the blanks by dilute sulphuric acid and sodium bichromate. Hot air is blown through other barrels into which the coin blanks have been placed to dry. More recently the gas-fired furnaces (called oxidising furnaces) have been replaced by bright annealing furnaces which produce clean blanks that do not need to be blanched.

19 Since medieval times sample coins have been placed in a locked wooden box, or pyx, and these are later examined by a jury of assayers. The coins are weighed carefully and are checked to ensure that they conform to standards of purity. The Trial of the Pyx is held annually at Goldsmiths' Hall in London

5 *Marking*. The blanks have the rim raised by rolling them under pressure along a narrow groove. This is called 'marking'. The rim is raised on coins so that they can be stacked in columns and so that the face of the coin is given some protection as it circulates.

6 *Striking*. Blanks are placed into trays from which the operator of the striking machine lifts them and puts them into the tube that leads to the part of the machine where the striking is done. The most modern machines are hopper-fed and so the feeding of blanks into the machine is continuous. The blanks drop down one at a time above the bottom die—usually the obverse of the coin—and the top die is squeezed on to it with a pressure of 250 tons for large coins. Older presses produced 120 coins a minute but the modern ones have more than doubled this output to 250 coins a minute.

7 *Inspection*. When they have been struck, the coins are placed on a moving belt and each coin is examined. Defective ones are removed. The coins that pass this examination are counted out—electronic 'tellers' automatically count out the correct number of coins to fill each bag. The machine then switches itself off and the machine operator moves the feeding channel to the next empty bag. The machine counts coins at the rate of seventeen a second.

8 *Weighing*. The metal is weighed on several occasions, partly for security purposes, and even the scrap metal is so checked. Bulk metals are weighed as they arrive at the factory; the cast bars are weighed and the strips of metal are weighed before being cut. The blanks are weighed into bags, and the coins are weighed on at least five further occasions.

9 *Assaying*. The Assay Department checks that the metals used to make coins are of the required purity and this involves testing the metals at certain points in the production process as well as examining the finished coins. Samples of coins are removed for assay tests, and coins are also tested annually by an independent jury at Goldsmiths' Hall. This latter test is known as the Trial of the Pyx.

Further reading
J. Hawthorne, *All About Money* (W. H. Allen)
F. Purvey, *Collecting Coins* (Foyle)
R. A. G. Carson, *Coins: Ancient, Mediaeval and Modern* (Hutchinson)
G. C. Brooke, *English Coins* (Methuen)
J. Craig, *The Mint* (CUP)

4 Paper Money

The first banknotes

The Chinese not only invented paper, they invented paper money also and the oldest banknotes in existence today are from China. Paper money was safer and easier to carry about than sackfuls of coin and it was to prevent constant robberies of coin that Emperor Hien Tsung began to use paper money made from mulberry bark and decorated with dragons and chrysanthemums. This money was termed Flying Money because it could be hidden in saddlebags and quickly sent on long journeys by using relays of horses.

It was the traveller Marco Polo who proclaimed in wonder, if inaccurately: 'The Great Khan has a means whereby he can have all the treasure of all the kings in the world by turning paper into gold.'

Banknotes were first issued briefly in Europe in Sweden in 1660, but when paper money came to be used in Britain it was introduced in stages. In the seventeenth century rich people began to realise the folly of hiding their gold in holes in walls or the ground. Surely some safer way could be devised to look after coins. The goldsmiths came up with the answer. Rich people started to deposit their money—and other valuables too—with goldsmiths who had safes to keep gold in for their own purposes and who usually charged for locking-up customers' money. Certificates were issued which gave customers the right to withdraw their coins whenever they chose. In one sense, these receipts were like our banknotes today, in that they promised to pay out on demand, but they were made out to a certain person and payable only to him, or to someone he named.

The goldsmiths soon realised that whilst some customers constantly brought money to be deposited in the bank, and others came to reclaim theirs, on balance there was always some money lying idle in the safe. This money could be given to people who required a loan, and they had to pay it back with interest. So the goldsmiths were only too keen to tout for customers to deposit money with them, and were willing to pay them for doing so, because out of the high rate of interest they charged for loans, they could afford to pay the depositors and still make a profit for themselves.

In time, the receipts issued by the goldsmiths were made out so that they could be paid out to the bearer—rather than to a named individual—and so these receipts could then be exchanged from person to person. They were, in fact, pieces of paper money, and by the year 1729 printed receipts were produced.

The Bank of England was founded in 1694 and £1,200,000 was provided to set it up by shareholders who received stock. The main aim initially of the newly-created bank was to raise money to continue the war with France, but the issuing

20 The banknote room at the Bank of England in the middle of the nineteenth century

of banknotes became one of its main responsibilities. At that time the Bank of England was the only bank in the world that was issuing notes.

Bank of England notes

The Bank of England first printed banknotes in 1695, ranging in denominations from £10 to £100 so it can be seen that these notes were not meant for ordinary people to handle. Each note had the bearer's name and the cashier's signature in handwriting as well as the date. The remainder of the note was copperplate printed. But these notes were fair game for forgers and within a few weeks a forged note for £100 had been discovered. Acts were passed to stop unauthorised persons from issuing notes (1697) and which allowed only organisations with six partners or less to issue notes (1709) which aimed at restricting the number of notes issued. The type of paper, the engraving and the watermark were all changed on various occasions, but the forgers continued to flourish. So many acts were passed making it illegal to forge banknotes, as in 1724 and 1763, that Blackstone, writing in 1768, said 'there is hardly now a case possible to be conceived wherein forgery, that tends to defraud, whether in the name of a real or fictitious person, is not made a capital crime'.

Convertible currency

Many private banks were opened in all parts of the country. Often they issued far too many banknotes and when customers became suspicious and thought that a certain bank could not change banknotes for gold, then everyone clamoured to try to change their notes before the bank's supply of gold ran out. Such a bank was often unable to change all the notes presented without warning and so it had to close. Many banks ended in failure. Confidence in a bank was of great importance and a rumour about a bank's inability to meet its issue of notes with gold might start a 'run on the bank', as it was known, with disastrous results. To restore confidence might be impossible and many banks had to close their doors, resulting in ruin for many people. It is important to remember that when Britain had a convertible currency (as opposed to the inconvertible currency of today) people could change their notes for supplies of gold—which had a permanent value of its own as a valuable metal—simply by handing their notes over the counter at a bank.

The first run on a bank occurred in 1704 when the Bank of Scotland closed its doors temporarily against customers because of its inability to cash notes for gold.

Banking was still essentially a local undertaking within any one district. A bad harvest in one locality, for instance, was often enough to cause people to panic and to start a run on the local banks. Many banks limited their issue of notes within reasonable bounds, but even these could not survive a fast rush to obtain metal in exchange for notes. Public lack of confidence was often widespread in

21 A £1,000 note dated 20 April 1934. There are now banknotes for £1, £5, £10 and £20 in England, and also £100 notes in Scotland and Ireland, although these are not legal tender in England. Higher values of banknotes have been rendered obsolete by the widespread use of cheques

22 This picture shows some of the anguish and panic of customers when a bank failed. In this case the run was on the Birkbeck Bank in Chancery Lane, London, in 1892

any district where trouble had occurred due to people withdrawing their gold and silver in panic. In Dublin, in 1754, three major banks closed when the partners of two absconded and the other closed because of fraud. Five banks were left in operation in the city but two of these closed soon afterwards in 1759; the panic was tremendous and the surviving three banks in Dublin managed to stay open, but only just.

Highway robbery was so rife in the eighteenth century that in 1738 the government issued Bank Post Bills which were paid out seven days after the date on which they were issued. This allowed travellers who had been held up and robbed by highwaymen or footpads to authorise that payment of the bills was withheld. The introduction of mail coaches, which carried an armed guard, effectively ended attacks on such long-distance traffic.

Sending banknotes by post was a risky business. Sometimes people cut a banknote in half and sent each half in separate letters, the recipient gluing the pieces together again. Rates of postage were high in Britain until the postal reforms of 1840 and one of the duties of post office clerks was to hold letters up to the light in order to discover how many sheets of paper a letter contained. Letters were charged according to the number of sheets, or enclosures, and not by weight as is the case today. A dishonest clerk could easily steal banknotes from letters in the course of his normal work.

In 1725 Bank of England notes were used for amounts varying from as much as £20 to £1,000. As we discovered in Chapter 3, there was a severe shortage of metal money in the eighteenth century and the issue of these banknotes was partly caused by this shortage.

Unlimited issues

During the reign of George III, which lasted from 1760 to 1820, gold coinage was more or less replaced by banknotes. Silver and copper coins were of very little importance as these metals became extremely costly. The lowest denomination

23 A guinea note (£1.05) dated 9 November 1809, from Greenock Bank Co.

42

of the Bank of England notes was still £10, but the private country banks provided £1 notes and these were used by the majority of people who thought in units and not in hundreds or thousands of pounds.

The number of banks issuing large numbers of notes was becoming extremely dangerous, and many others besides the banks issued notes. Such issues became a popular pastime. Builders, shopkeepers, butchers, bakers—and quite possibly candlestick makers too—issued their own notes. Some of these were for very small amounts. The Fort Montague note for five half-pence showed a picture of a fort over which flew a Union Jack. Fort Montague was, in fact, a tea shop in Yorkshire with a total capital of about £13!

Besides banks and firms, individuals even issued their own notes and this was quite legal. All that was needed was a certain amount of local confidence within which the notes could circulate. The forger had a hey-day with such a multiplicity of notes to choose from, and in 1775 notes of less than £1 were banned by Act of Parliament. In 1777 the smallest note allowed was the £5 one.

Banks today are allowed to issue notes in excess of their capital holdings only to strictly laid-down limits, and so it is difficult for us to understand just how risky banking was in the eighteenth and early nineteenth centuries, when many banks issued banknotes greatly in excess of their capital. Banks relied entirely on the fact that in all probability many notes would always be held by customers and that at no time would all the notes be presented for cashing into gold or silver. One bank was founded by four people, each of whom put in £500. Weeks later they had issued notes to the value of about £14,000. Within twenty years, although their capital had increased by only £8,000, their note issue had risen to £180,000.

The Bank Restriction Act

The Bank of England first issued £5 notes in 1793, the year in which the Napoleonic Wars broke out, in the hope that people would hold £5 notes instead of gold. Shortage of gold became acute as the war progressed and within a couple of years the Bank of England also issued notes of £100, £200, £300 and £500 for the same purpose. Many people, however, felt happier to hold gold in such an unsettled period and a raid by French troops on the coast of Wales encouraged unfounded rumours of an invasion. Conditions became so inflamed that the directors of the Bank of England were ordered by the government to stop cash payments for a time to prevent an inevitable run on the Bank of England. The Bank Restriction Act came into force which restricted payment of gold or silver by the Bank of England and so Britain had an inconvertible currency down to 1820. New notes were issued and, for the first time, the Bank of England issued £1 and £2 notes in 1797. Private country banks also issued notes of these low values now that restrictions on their use had been lifted.

The numbers of country banks continued to increase. Within the twelve years ending in 1810, the number of country banks rose from 270 to 720. These banks had a total country note issue of thirty million pounds. But forgery became rife again. Many people were in possession of £1 and £2 notes who had never before handled paper money and would find great difficulty in detecting forgeries from genuine notes. Indeed, at times the Bank of England itself had been unable to identify its own notes as being genuine!

By the year 1817 about 31,000 forged notes were in existence, all of them made from only a few engravings. In that year more than thirty people were hanged for passing forged notes—only these people and not the makers were arrested. Over three hundred people had been hanged for this offence within twenty years and George Cruikshank fought hard to change the harshness of the law. It became a common sight in London to see men or women hanging from gibbets outside Newgate Prison. Hanging resulted if a person was found passing even one forged £1 note. The death sentence for this crime was abolished in 1832, which was also an important year of reform in other spheres.

A shortage of gold

After the end of hostilities with France, £1 and £2 country banknotes were discontinued in 1821 as were Bank of England £2 notes. At first, supplies of gold were adequate without having to resort to notes of such low values, but, inevitably, the supply of gold began to dwindle. Some of it was sent abroad and other gold coin was absorbed throughout the country. Danger began to loom ahead but it was not foreseen by banking authorities in London. In 1822 five hundred country banks, many of them small, speculative businesses, were given the right to issue £1 notes of unlimited quantities, and in four years the number of banknotes doubled to eight million. The public often requested gold in exchange for these notes, and the supply of gold coin became depleted in country banks. 1825 was a dangerous year and the Bank of England ran short of gold and even of its own £1 notes, which were regarded as safer than notes of the country banks, since notes from country banks could be exchanged for gold or for Bank of England notes. The Bank of England was saved when a collection of its own £1 notes was found hidden in the vaults and one of the directors of the Bank admitted 'They worked wonders; one box containing a quantity of one-pound notes had been overlooked, and they were forthcoming at the lucky moment. As far as my judgment goes, it saved the credit of the country'.

Before the end of 1825 many banks had closed in London and in the rest of the country. Within a matter of days more than sixty country banks and six important London banks had closed their doors. The government bought gold from anyone who had it to sell and so stocked up on the low gold reserves. The Mint worked hard to make coin from gold bars, and so worse trouble still was avoided. In 1826 notes under £5 were prohibited, and so the Bank of England £1 notes of 1797 were no longer used.

Cheques, as we now know them, were first used in 1825. Many people were suspicious of them at first and their introduction was gradual but, as people

24 Soiled and torn banknotes being burned under supervision in a furnace at the Bank of England in 1872

became used to the safety of cheques and their greater convenience for the transfer of money, more of them were used where before money itself had passed hands.

The Bank Charter Act, 1844

There was no proper banking system for the whole country and still far too many small, inefficient banks in existence, which made banking a precarious business. In 1844 Sir Robert Peel brought in the Bank Charter Act which restricted the activities of unsuitable banking enterprises, and which gave to the Bank of England a monopoly to issue banknotes within 65 miles (105 km) of London. The aim of this important Act was to regulate the banking system of the country and to cut down on the use of bank credit. The number of banknotes which could be issued was determined by the amount of gold held at the Bank of England. In addition, up to fourteen million pounds in notes could be issued against securities. Apart from the Bank of England, only country banks already issuing

45

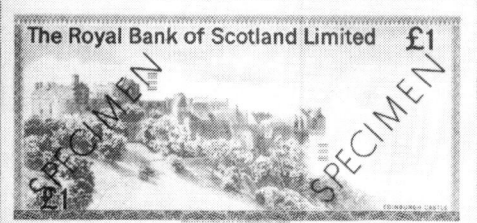

25 A set of new Scottish banknotes was issued by The Royal Bank of Scotland Ltd in 1972, and these notes have pictures of Scottish castles on the reverse. Two of them are shown here

notes in 1844 could now issue notes, and these banks were restricted to the total number of notes already being printed. If a bank became insolvent or was taken over by another bank, its right of note issue lapsed. Naturally, these new rules were disliked by the country banks who found that their activities were severely restricted, but the plan began to work as had been anticipated for in the decade after 1844 thirty-seven banks were forced to close. Of course, these measures meant that even more Bank of England notes than formerly now circulated and were used in place of the country banknotes which were very much reduced in number.

We must not suppose that the 1844 Act gave anything like a monopoly to the Bank of England in the issue of banknotes throughout the country as a whole. On the contrary, there were 279 banks allowed to issue their own notes, but this number gradually dwindled as the nineteenth century progressed. By 1900 sixty English banks still issued their own notes. In 1921 the last bank of these sixty—Fox, Fowler and Co of Wellington—ceased to issue its own notes when it amalgamated with Lloyds Bank. In 1845 another Act of Parliament was passed to regulate the issue of banknotes in Scotland and Ireland. The 1844 Act had enforced regulations only in England and Wales.

The Bank Act of 1844 was the basis on which English banking has grown into modern times. On three separate occasions in the nineteenth century the Bank Act had to be suspended because of crisis. In 1847, during the period of railway mania, cash reserves at the Bank of England were very low and so the Bank was given permission to issue more notes than the number it was limited to issue in normal times, but the Bank did not need to make use of this right. In 1866 when the threat of war in Europe resulted in the crash of several financial firms, the Bank Act was again suspended, but, as in 1847, it did not avail itself of the temporary right to issue uncovered notes. Between these crises, in 1857, there was a third financial crisis and to restore confidence the Bank of England did, on this one occasion, exceed the note issue.

The Bank Act was suspended for the fourth time in 1914 on the outbreak of the First World War when the Bank of England's gold reserves were very low. In the same year the Currency and Bank Notes Act introduced new £1 and 10s (50p) notes, and for a limited period postal orders too were used as currency until the monetary system had time to adjust to the demands of the country. Postal orders, as such, had been in use since 1880 when they were printed on the printing machines belonging to the Bank of England. By 1905 there were forty-one denominations of postal orders, and by 1910 one hundred and thirty-two million postal orders were issued yearly. The reader will be sufficiently well-acquainted with the use of postal orders to understand their value as a means of sending money safely through the post.

The effects of two World Wars
When the Allies declared war on Germany early in August 1914 the banks remained closed for a few days and so did the Stock Exchange. When the banks reopened, people were amazingly calm and a dangerous situation was saved by public confidence in the banking system. People accepted banknotes freely, and gold hardly circulated at all. Many people were hanging on to the gold coins which they possessed already, probably expecting that sovereigns would rise in value compared with banknotes and so it was made an offence to melt down coins. 2½ million £1 Treasury notes were issued quickly but there was no need to issue unbacked notes, though the Bank Charter Act had been suspended just in case.

£1 and 10s (50p) notes were subsequently printed in various issues. The last of these temporary issues were printed in 1928 in green (£1) and brown (10s) and were called banknotes and not 'Treasury notes' as were the first of these issues. The first temporary issues had been issued by the Treasury because 'banknotes' for values of under £5 were not legal.

Issues of notes valued at £1, 10s (50p), 5s (25p), and 2s 6d (12½p) were prepared for use during the Second World War but the last two denominations were not used. From May 1945 higher value banknotes (those of £10 and more) were no longer legal tender, and from March 1946 the same ruling applied to £5 notes which were dated earlier than September 1944. This measure was to simplify the issue of notes in war-time and to make things difficult for people who attempted to break currency regulations. But another reason for these steps was to prevent German forgeries of English banknotes from playing havoc in Britain. A Bank of England cashier happened to notice two notes with the same number and this alerted the authorities to the dangers of forgery. The German government put together all the Jewish counterfeiters in Germany—more than a hundred of them—into Sachsenhausen concentration camp. Their job was to produce English money for the Germans. The counterfeited issue of the white £5 note was so good that a Bank of England expert was needed to identify them. More than £100,000,000 in forged notes was produced. Fortunately, many were destroyed but some filtered into England. Had the original plan worked, and millions of notes been circulated in England, the economy would have been ruined.

In fact, England made forged German 50 *pfennig* notes and these were dropped into Germany; some of them had anti-Hitler rhymes printed on the reverse side.

After hostilities ended in 1945, new £5 notes were issued which had a metal thread, first introduced in notes in 1939, running through the paper. This is a security measure to make forgery difficult. New notes were issued in 1948 and there have been several new issues since.

The £1 and 10s (50p) notes of 1960 and 1961 respectively, included, as something of an innovation, a picture of the Queen instead of Britannia. From 1961 the old black and white £5 notes ceased to be legal tender.

Manufacturing banknotes

The firm of Portals makes all the special paper on which English banknotes are printed, and the Bank of England—obviously having a considerable interest in a continuous supply of security paper—owns a fair number of Portals' shares. Portals have supplied the Bank of England with paper for banknotes since 1724, from soon after the Bank was formed, when Henri Portal, a French refugee, first supplied watermarked paper to the Bank. Portals supply security paper to more than 100 countries, the Bank of England buying less than a third of all the security paper that the firm produces.

Coins survive much longer than pieces of paper money, of course, and so far fewer early banknotes are available for the student and the collector than early coins, though museums often contain samples. Pieces of paper that are constantly being folded up and passed from hand to hand naturally survive for short periods only. The old 10s (50p) notes were unfit for use after only six months in service. One pound notes generally last for about eight months to a year before they need to be destroyed; but some are unfit for use in a still shorter time. If you visit a bank you may notice the clerk putting aside any dirty or torn notes when he counts out notes from a pile of money. Notes that are unfit for circulation are returned to the Bank of England's printing works at Debden in Essex and destroyed in furnaces. The heat produced provides hot water to the building and also warmth— perhaps the most expensive form of central heating yet devised!

The production of paper money is a major operation all of which is undertaken at the printing works at Debden. Millions of new notes for use in Britain are printed every day. Even so, the demand increases faster than the supply. Britain's demand for new banknotes is curiously large, far larger than West Germany's, for instance, which is a country of similar size. For about twelve weeks in the year the commercial banks are not able to pay out any new notes to customers, who must accept used ones during those weeks. This is an attempt to get more life out of the notes already in circulation.

About 1,600 people work at the printing works at Debden where security precautions are rigorous. In the past, notes were printed on large single sheets of paper each of which had twenty-four notes printed on it. These had then to be cut apart by machine. Now long reels of paper pass into the printing machines and the operation is continuous—in much the same way as a modern newspaper is printed.

A torn banknote, or one that is partly missing, can be changed at a bank or post office for a new one if more than half the original note exists and if several other requirements are fulfilled—the words 'promise to pay' must be there, part

26 A cheque sorting machine. There are also machines able to count several hundred banknotes a minute, and others which weigh packets of coins to save cashiers counting one by one

of the signature and at least one complete number. A note which consists of less than this must be sent to the Bank of England with an explanation of what happened to the original note. Perhaps surprisingly, fifty men and women work in one department in Threadneedle Street and do nothing but examine the remains of notes that have been burnt, bleached, eaten or even dry-cleaned. Several millions of notes are claimed each year and customers receive whole notes in their place. Even a pile of charred paper will be examined carefully and the money will be replaced if the value of the claim is found to be genuine.

In fig. 21 you can see a Bank of England note for £1,000. In fact, there are even several one million pound notes in existence, written by hand on parchment in the early nineteenth century, and these are locked in the Bank of England and only used internally for accounting.

Our notes are changed every so often—a new £5 note was issued in 1971— and a new design, colour and size is used. Recently collecting banknotes as a hobby has been given an impetus and books on this subject are now available. Old notes can be very valuable to collectors. An eighteenth-century £10 note now costs over £150 to buy from a dealer. A mint (unused) 1967 10s (50p) note costs more than a pound. Many foreign notes can be bought quite cheaply and an interesting collection can be formed for a modest expense.

In some countries banknotes are issued for values of only a few pence. It seems surprising to the British to visit such countries as Romania, .for instance, and to have to hand over to a bus conductor several pieces of paper money for even a short bus ride—and to get no change!

Further reading
C. Narbeth, *Collecting Paper Money* (Lutterworth)

5 The Work of Banks

In London banking began in the middle ages with the activities of groups of people—such as the goldsmiths—who carried out many of the functions of banks as we know them. They accepted deposits, issued receipts that could be used as banknotes and made loans. In the provinces, banks grew out of merchant and manufacturing interests. Samuel Lloyd was a Birmingham ironmaster and Barclay was a linen draper. There were nearly four hundred private country banks by the end of the eighteenth century.

The Bank of England was the only joint-stock bank in the country until the nineteenth century. Joint-stock companies are owned by various people jointly, each of whom own some of the shares of the firm. The Act of 1826 allowed joint-stock banking and such banks began on a sound basis with more capital than banks that were privately owned. Many leading banks began life soon after 1826. From 1833 joint-stock banks were allowed to open in London if they did not issue banknotes. Banks began to merge into groups that could help each other and withstand a run on a certain bank in the group. Amalgamation grew apace and some private banks became joint-stock: Lloyds and Barclays are two examples. Since the end of the First World War further amalgamation has occurred and by 1921 the 'Big Five' were in existence: Midland, Barclays, Lloyds, National Provincial and Westminster. National Provincial and Westminster were linked as National Westminster in 1968 and since then further mergers have taken place. Now there are the 'Big Four' as well as two smaller banks in England. In Scotland there are now only three banks.

This chapter will show some of the main jobs a bank does today and show the importance of different kinds of banks, all of which exist both to make money and to provide essential services. Different kinds of banks exist to provide specialised facilities and so it will be helpful to list these types of banks and to comment briefly on their functions.

27 The huge growth of business transactions has resulted in banks becoming dependent on computer calculations for the processing of accounts. When a new account is opened at a branch the particulars are entered on punch-cards at the head office of the bank

28 Older banks are being updated in the appearance of the buildings and new branches are light, spacious and comfortable. Many post offices and banks, like this one, now have protective window shields between customers and counter staff

Types of banks

The Bank of England is the central bank of the country and since the Bank of England Act of 1946 it has been a public institution. The Bank of England is the Government's bank and exchanges advice and information with the Government. It is largely self-governing, controls the monetary system and also issues banknotes. It is directed by experts, each of whom represents important sectors of the economy —shipping, commerce and industry, for instance—and these people are appointed to serve because of their detailed knowledge in certain fields. The other banks in England all have accounts at the Bank of England which now has hardly any private customers.

The *merchant banks* finance international trading.

A further group comprises the head offices of British Overseas and Commonwealth Banks, and London Branches of other Overseas Banks.

In the *Trustee Savings Banks* ten million depositors leave their savings and earn interest on the deposits. These banks began in Scotland more than one hundred years ago and soon were started in England. They are local banks, organised by

29 The Clearing House at the Bank of England in the nineteenth century

paid officials and with unpaid boards of trustees; most of the latter are well-known people locally. Much of the money deposited is lent to the Government; the remainder is invested. An account with a Trustee Savings Bank does not bring with it a cheque book, but the bank will provide a cheque for a customer on request.

The National Savings Bank began as the Post Office Savings Bank in 1861. Money deposited in the National Savings Bank, through local post offices, is invested in Government stocks. Savings banks are, therefore, means by which the Government can borrow money from the public as well as encouraging the habit of saving. The amount that can be deposited is limited as these accounts are meant for people saving small sums of money. Larger amounts can be invested in savings certificates, bonds and premium bonds.

The Post Office Giro banking service began in 1968 to provide a quick and cheap way of transferring money for people without a bank account. The Giro service transfers credit from one account-holder to the account of another holder. Payments can be made in safety by post as money itself is not sent, and a record of all payments made is retained.

Possibly most important for many people are the *commercial joint-stock banks*.

30 This Chubb strongroom door has an overall thickness of 42 inches (95 cm), and an effective thickness of 30 inches (75 cm). It weighs 30 tons. Many strongroom doors have four combination locks, each of which has one hundred million code changes. The doors are often fitted with a time lock device

There are branches of these banks in all towns and even in large villages all over the country. They are registered public companies that are owned by many shareholders. These banks are known by their names—Barclays, Midland, Lloyds, National Westminster (the Big Four) and two others: Coutts, and Williams & Glyn's.

A commercial bank provides many ancillary services for the benefit of its customers, some of which will be mentioned later in this chapter, but such banks have four main purposes: they accept on deposit money from customers, they collect and transfer money throughout the country and the world, they lend money to customers and they distribute banknotes and coins throughout the country.

Bank accounts

There are various types of bank accounts and a customer is able to have one or more of these different kinds. Many people have only a current account and if a pay cheque from the employer is paid direct to the bank it will go into the customer's account. A customer with a current account is given a cheque book and he can then write cheques authorising the bank to pay out a sum of money from his account. Cheques are convenient pieces of paper. They can be issued by the bank crossed or open. A crossed cheque has two lines running through it and, if it is being paid to a firm, the words '& Co' written on it (all of which can also be put in by hand, so changing an open cheque into a crossed cheque). The advantage of a crossed cheque is that it must be paid into an account and cannot

31 A Bank of England £5 note which has survived from 1793. This was the first year in which Bank of England £5 notes were issued. Certain parts of the note had to be filled in by hand

32 Cheques are sorted and returned cancelled by some commercial banks to the customer who wrote them in the first place. These can be retained by the customers for reference or simply be destroyed

simply be cashed over the counter, like an open cheque. So if a crossed cheque is stolen and a thief tries to cash it he can be easily traced. An advantage of both kinds of cheque is that they can be written for any odd amount which is easier than finding banknotes and coins for such specific amounts as, for example, £7.96.

Suppose Mr Brown writes a cheque asking his bank to pay £10 to Mr Smith's current account at the same bank, the transaction is simply a matter of debiting Mr Brown's account and crediting that of Mr Smith. No money need change hands—only a book ledger transaction is made. But in practice things are not quite so simple for there are thousands of banks and millions of cheques. Someone with a current account with Barclays may receive a cheque written by someone with an account at Midland Bank. Most cheques written by customers with accounts at Barclays, for instance, will inevitably be written in favour of customers with accounts at other banks. To sort out these huge numbers of cheques is a gigantic task which is undertaken by the Clearing House. When Mr Simpson receives a £20 cheque from his aunt who lives in another city, he pays the cheque

33 Chester House at Wimbledon, Surrey, is the Staff Training Centre for Barclays Bank. Many banks have such colleges where staff attend lectures and discussions on the business of running a bank. Some of these colleges are residential

into his current account which is then increased by the value of the cheque, but the cheque must be sent by the bank to be cleared. All cheques are sent to the Clearing House in London where they are sorted into bundles for individual cities. Each bundle of cheques is then returned to the city from which the cheques were issued, and these are sub-divided into smaller bundles, one bundle for each bank. The bank reduces Mr Smith's aunt's account by £20 and then cancels the cheque by stamping the word 'paid' on it so that it cannot be used again.

The commercial banks all have accounts at the Bank of England. Any difference in the total value of the cheques paid out and received from one commercial bank to another can be balanced by a cheque drawn on that bank's account at the Bank of England. The Bank of England then deducts the relevant amount from the reserve of one commercial bank and adds it to the reserve of another bank. No movement of banknotes or coins takes place.

A customer with a current account receives no interest from the bank for allowing his money to remain there until he needs it. Cheques are being written all the time and a customer's current account changes daily as amounts are added to or subtracted from it. Indeed, the bank probably makes a charge for providing this service.

If a customer decides to leave his money in an account for a reasonably long period, naturally he wishes the money to make interest for him. In this case he chooses a deposit account, and many people have a current account, and also a deposit account, the latter of which they use for savings. The bank likes to know seven days in advance if a customer wants to withdraw money from a deposit account. If a customer has only a deposit account he is not provided with a cheque book.

Banks also have a savings account which is similar to the deposit account but the money is withdrawable without giving the bank warning. Savings accounts are meant for small savers and the rate of interest is less than in the deposit account.

Bank loans

The money that customers deposit in a bank does not all remain there, of course. Only enough is kept to meet likely demands for cash from customers. Extra cash that is not needed by customers is kept at the Head Offices of the bank and also each bank has an account at the Bank of England. Other money is lent or invested. Often banks do not lend money for very long periods as depositors may wish to be paid back at any time. Loans are often reviewed each year. Banks provide finance for industry, agriculture and trading as well as giving loans and overdrafts to private customers. They also lend money to the Government by buying Treasury Bills from the money market. They invest in Government securities and also lend for very short periods to financial institutions in the City of London. Often a 'very short period' may be one night only.

Banks earn interest from these enterprises and with the money that is earned they maintain premises, pay staff and other expenses and provide the means for transferring and collecting money.

The cash that a bank keeps in its counter tills and the money it has in its Bank of England account are thought of as 'cash' and add up to about 8 per cent of the bank's total deposits. This is known as the cash ratio. The other 92 per cent of a bank's deposits is used in the ways outlined above. The cash ratio and part of the other 92 per cent—the money available to the bank 'at call' (at once) or on 'short notice' (within three days to a week)—together are termed the liquidity ratio. A liquidity ratio of 30 per cent simply means that about one-third of a bank's deposits are sufficiently 'liquid' or 'available' in a short period should

34 A branch bank at Gatwick Airport, London, for the convenience of customers who are travelling abroad or arriving in this country

customers suddenly demand cash. Other loans made by the bank can be tied up for much longer periods. The longer the period before the loan need be repaid the more illiquid the money is said to be. When a bank holds a great deal of liquid cash it does not earn much interest on its loans. On the other hand, if a bank has much illiquid cash it may not be able to satisfy its depositors when they demand repayment. The ratio of types of loans to deposits therefore is of considerable importance and a reasonable balance must be maintained.

Banks are said to create money when they grant a loan because they increase the amount of deposits as a whole. Suppose someone asked a bank manager to lend him £1,000. If the customer can offer some security—such as a life assurance policy—just in case he falls behind in his repayment, then the bank may agree to a loan. Of course, if all the depositors at a bank decided suddenly to demand their savings in cash then the bank manager would be in trouble, but in settled times this emergency never happens and the bank knows that it can make loans and receive a good rate of interest on them. If the Government decides that people should spend less money the banks are forced to raise their liquidity ratio so that they can make fewer long-term loans. It is made more difficult for people to borrow from banks and rates of interest on repayment can be raised.

Other institutions besides banks have grown in importance over the years and these also lend money. Building societies make loans to customers to enable them to buy a home and they also provide saving facilities. Finance houses lend money for hire-purchase business and insurance companies also lend money.

Other facilities

There are many other services which banks provide for their customers. Banks have large strongrooms and safes where money is stored, and customers may leave important documents—such as Share Certificates, Deeds and Wills—in safe-keeping in a bank's strong room. Boxes and parcels of valuables may also be left. Some banks have safe deposit facilities with private compartments for customers who require this service.

Probably you have noticed night safes on the outside walls of banks which allow customers such as shopkeepers who cannot get to the bank before it closes to deposit their money safely. The customer has a wallet in which he puts the money and a key to open the night safe.

Some banks have a cash dispenser on the outside wall which contains packets of £10 in notes. The customer has a card which he places into the machine after tapping a personal number on the keyboard. This releases a packet of notes. Cash dispensers are useful when banks are closed at night, at weekends and particularly over holiday periods.

People intending to travel abroad can obtain foreign money and traveller's cheques from banks. People with a lot of money often have the bank act as trustee or adviser, and banks also act as executor of estates when people die. Periodic payments which come regularly such as subscriptions, hire purchase instalments,

35 This mobile branch bank visits customers in lonely areas near Whitby in the North Riding of Yorkshire

life assurance premiums and mortgage repayments will be made by the bank if the customer signs a standing order asking the bank to make these payments when they fall due. Many people use credit cards to prevent the risk of losing their money and also for convenience, and these will be discussed in the final chapter of this book.

Banks provide a great variety of services, including confidential advice, and their role in the community is a very important one. It is unfortunate that when people are robbed at home of their savings, which some old people especially tend to keep hidden under mattresses and inside old teapots, they often say that they don't trust banks. The writer Mark Twain insisted that 'a banker is a fellow

36 (*left*) Many branch banks have a night safe on the outside wall. Shopkeepers and others who find it difficult to deposit money in the bank before it closes in the afternoon, can pay a nominal charge and are provided with a wallet and a key to the night safe. Banks will provide customers with two kinds of lockable wallets. The brown wallet can only be opened by the depositor on the following morning. The black wallet is opened the next morning by two members of the bank staff and the money is paid into the account of the depositor, who encloses a deposit slip in the wallet with the money. When the door of the night safe is closed, the wallets drop down into a safe—not the strongroom—where they are kept safely until morning who lends you his umbrella when the sun is shining and wants it back the minute it begins to rain'. But most people now realise that their money is most secure when it is deposited in a bank or in a building society, where it is safe from theft and where it is able to earn them interest. Banks are friendly places where new customers are always welcomed and are assured of help and good advice however small the amount of money they deposit.

Further reading
J. Dandy, *Your Money and Its Life* (Hutchinson)
Study booklets 1–12 (Bank Education Service)

37 (*opposite*) Cash dispensers are now being fitted outside banks and these provide customers with cash at any time, so they are particularly useful after the banks have closed, at weekends and over holiday periods. A customer obtains vouchers from his bank which he keeps for emergency use when he needs to obtain money outside of banking hours. He presses button C on the cash dispenser and then his own six figure number. He opens the drawer, puts a voucher inside and closes the drawer. A 'Wait' sign lights up. Then the 'Accepted' light comes on and he opens the drawer again, takes out £10 in notes and closes the drawer. A customer whose branch bank does not have a cash dispenser installed can still obtain vouchers and use them at other branches of that bank. Lloyds Bank call their cash dispensing service 'Readycash' and Barclays Bank call it 'Barclaycash'

6 Money in the Economy

The cash flow

An important service provided by the banks for the whole community is the movement of bank notes and coins around the country. Notes and coins must be constantly moved from places where there is a surplus and taken to places where they are required more urgently. Sometimes it is especially important to preserve an even cash flow during holiday seasons. In the summer, much money is spent at seaside resorts and this means a depletion of money in nearby towns. At Christmas a great deal of money is spent in city shops and this leaves many suburban housing areas without adequate cash for normal use. But apart from seasonal flows of money in certain directions, there is a constant, never-ending need to ensure that all areas are provided with the cash needed for everyday use. For example, the wages paid to factory workers in a large plant may come from one bank but will be spent over a much wider area, so leaving the area in which payment was made short of cash.

38 The Bank of England in the late eighteenth century. It began operating in 1695 in the Grocers' Hall, Poultry. The foundations of the building in Threadneedle Street were laid in 1734, and many subsequent additions and alterations were made

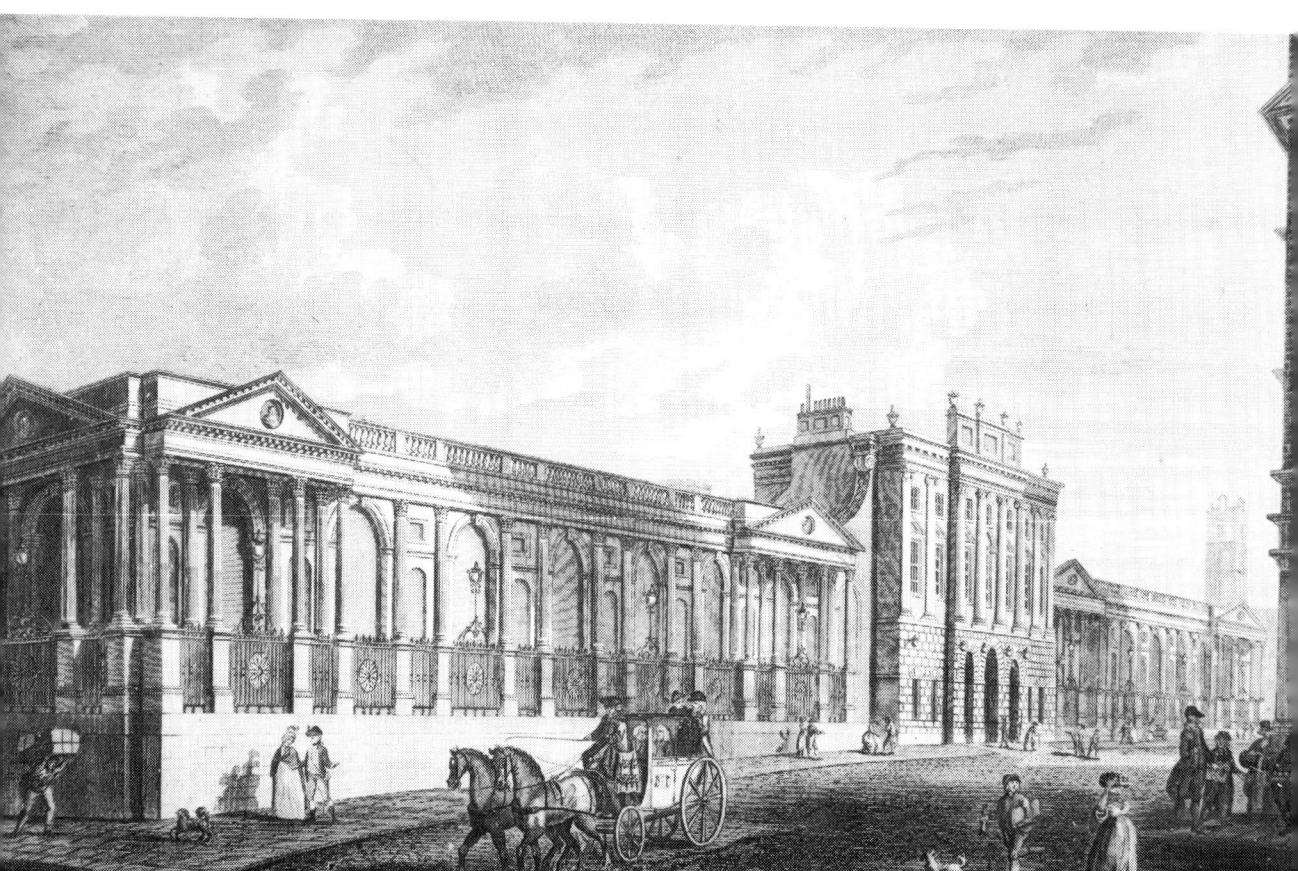

39 The Public Drawing Office in the Bank of England in Threadneedle Street, London, earlier in this century when the Bank of England—like the commercial banks today—had many private customers

The banks have the responsibility for seeing that currency is available in sufficient amounts in all parts of the country because money invariably finds its way through the banking system again and again as it is put to use by so many different people. It might appear that the simplest way to ensure that everywhere has enough cash would be to overstock each branch bank with notes and coins and to keep replenishing these supplies when they ran low. But this would mean that a huge amount of money would always lie unused in the bank strongrooms when it could be put to work in so many ways to make profits. In fact, branch banks do not like to have too much money lying idle in their strongrooms and so they estimate weekly how much cash they are likely to need to meet customer demands. As we discovered in the chapter on the work of banks, each bank is constantly paying out cash to customers and also receiving cash from other customers. Some branch banks in industrial areas which pay out many wages will pay out regularly more notes and coins than they receive, and these branches need extra cash sent in weekly to cater for the large demands made on them. Other branches receive more coins and notes than they are required to pay out. A branch in a busy shopping area is likely to receive a great deal of money from local shopkeepers. Such banks build up currency that is surplus to their needs and some of it is transferred to their central supply source. It is, of course, rare for a bank to be in a position where cash demanded and cash received tend to

40 The Court Room, Bank of England, where an important rate called the 'last resort rate' is fixed each week. This rate is related to the level of interest rates prevailing at the time in the money market. When the Government makes changes in the last resort rate, this influences other interest rates throughout the country and so makes borrowing and lending cheaper or dearer

balance exactly against each other. More usually, each branch manager needs to estimate how much money either to return to the central supply of money for that bank or how much money he needs to be sent to cope with customer demands. Moving coins and notes is expensive, but branches are able to receive or get rid of cash as local conditions dictate. Some banks have a central bullion department sited at the head office; others have local cash depots placed in different parts of the country. Cash is moved by road, rail and post as well as by security carriers. Bank notes are often sent by registered post but this is an expensive way to transport money. Of course, all money in transit—however it is being transported —is insured against loss. As more and more people use cheques, bank Giro credits and direct debits, the costs of transporting huge quantities of notes and coin are further reduced. But cash is still needed for many daily purposes and it is the job of the banks to see that it is in the right place at the right time.

Transporting money

Robberies of money in transit occur more frequently than the banks would like, and the risk of heavy loss is reduced by arrangements between local banks to exchange surplus cash and by the establishment of regional bullion centres. The banks are conscious of the risks involved in moving money from place to place—the Great Train Robbery is a reminder of the lengths to which thieves will go—and increased use is being made of the services offered by security carrier companies, of which *Securicor* is the best-known name throughout the world.

Securicor was founded in 1935 and has more than 170 branches in the British Isles as well as overseas in countries as far apart as Zambia, Hong Kong, Kenya, Norway and Malta. The organisation provides guards who are trained to protect valuables which are transported in specially constructed armoured cars. The firm has the largest fleet of security vehicles in the world and transports more than £20,000,000,000 each year. Securicor provide a wide range of services, each of

41 Securicor guards provide a twenty-four hour service in the transport of money and other valuables

42 Security guards delivering a consignment of money to a bank. Notice the special carrying case with the inside security lid

which results in greater safety and convenience for the valuables of individuals and firms.

Securicor collect money from the bank for firms and also deliver money to the bank. This saves the firm from sending a cashier and perhaps a bodyguard. It is safer and more efficient. Securicor provide a twenty-four hour service; if necessary, they collect cash late at night and deposit it in night safes or even hold the cash in their own vaults overnight.

Though increasing numbers of people are paid by cheque, a great many still receive cash in a wage packet. Preparing large numbers of wage packets takes a considerable length of time for a firm at the close of each week. Securicor have a wage packeting service and will carry money from the bank, prepare the wage packets and deliver these to the firm at exactly the time it requests them. For firms who wish to dispense entirely with payroll problems, Securicor associate with computer bureaux which prepare individual programmes and then compile wage slips. Securicor collect this information and its wage packeting department makes up the wage packets from the pay sheets.

For a firm that has to pay out wages at various factories, branches or sites, the danger of theft is greater. Securicor will collect the money for them by presenting the firm's cheque for the relevant amount at the bank. They sort and packet this money and then deliver it to the employees in armoured cars that have bandit-proof pay-out windows.

Theft often occurs when a firm or shop stores its daily takings overnight and then makes a regular morning bank deposit. Securicor will transport money to the bank and also empty parking meters and vending machines. Many smaller safes present few problems to experienced thieves, and Securicor services reduce considerably the danger of keeping money on the premises during the night.

Another service is the collection of packets of valuable goods that are to go by registered post. Securicor collect these, take them to the Post Office and then return the official receipt to the sender.

This range of services extends to more than the protection of money. Important documents can be stored by Securicor in their Chubb thief-resistant vaults.

43 A new service is the packing of coins into rolls which are simpler and cleaner to handle than loose coins. The loose coins in this picture are made up of £1.75 in mixed bronze. The three rolls of money also contain this amount: there is a £1 roll of 2p coins, a 50p roll of 1p coins and a 25p roll of ½p coins

Documents are returned to the client on demand. Other valuables are transported by the Securicor Armoured Division. Such things as paintings, jewels and drugs travel from place to place safely and reliably.

The company also provides customers with the right change at the right time. A telephone call is sufficient to obtain coins of the value required.

Finally, an important development which is likely to become of great value in the future is the coin processing service. Securicor have equipment which takes mixed cupro-nickel and bronze coins in quantity and sorts them. The coins are then counted into bags or wrapped in rolls. Wrapped coins are packed into boxes and take up far less space than bulky bags and sacks of coins.

Investment

So far in this chapter money has been examined moving through the country performing specific functions as part of the general job of keeping the economy moving. For any economy to flourish, it is important that money should be put to effective use. If Mr Brown keeps £100 in his desk drawer, the money is not being used as fully as it might be. Placed in a deposit account at the bank or in a building society it would at once start to earn the owner interest because the bank or building society can lend it at a higher rate of interest to someone who wishes to use it—perhaps to buy a house, to expand a business or to develop a new one. Money put to work in this way is a fundamental part of economic life.

Large enterprises have grown so big and important because they are owned by many people, some of them small savers, each of whom holds some of the shares in the company. In fact, many people are shareholders indirectly in some company or other without even realising it. People who save money through an insurance company often hold shares indirectly because insurance companies invest large amounts of the money they receive from savers. Similarly, the banks invest money in Government stock.

The Stock Exchange

There are different kinds of markets—all of which exist to buy and sell—from the street trader's stall to the supermarket, from the small grocery shop at the corner of the street to the Stock Exchange in London. In the Stock Exchange shares in companies are bought and sold. The fact that shares can be sold easily tends to encourage people to invest in them in the first place; they know that if they need to sell them eventually a buyer can always be found.

Anyone who wants to buy or sell shares in a public company instructs a broker who is a member of the London Stock Exchange. The broker contacts a jobber who specialises in shares of particular kinds. If a broker wants to buy shares for a client he asks the jobber to quote a price for the particular stock, but he does not tell the jobber if his customer wants to buy or sell it. The jobber gives him two prices. The higher price is his selling price and the lower one is his buying price. An agreement is made on the spot and these agreements are binding on the jobber. The motto on the Stock Exchange coat of arms is 'My word is my bond'. There is a gallery at the London Stock Exchange in Throgmorton Street where the public can watch the members of the Stock Exchange at work. The members on the 'floor' seem merely to wander round talking to each other, but a conversation of only a few seconds might result in the change of ownership of shares valued at a few pounds or at many thousands of pounds.

Members jot down notes of agreements they have made. The same day, brokers send Contract Notes to clients confirming what has been bought or sold and stating the price, the broker's commission and the stamp duty.

Banks often provide shares for customers or arrange to sell shares which customers have for sale. The banks deal with a stockbroker on behalf of the customer. This is often more convenient for the customer who lives far from London or from any other city which has a stock exchange.

People buy shares because they hope to make a profit from having them and because they have the confidence of knowing that if necessary they can always sell their shares in the future, though, of course, they know the price they get for them may be lower or higher than the original buying price. But transferring shares is a straightforward job. Both the seller and the buyer have to sign a Share Transfer form. Then the buyer receives a certificate which states how many shares in the company are now his.

The shares offered for sale on the Stock Exchange include shares in public companies as well as securities issued by British and foreign governments and also shares issued by local authorities. The shares of private companies cannot be offered to the general public and cannot be transferred to another holder without the consent of the other shareholders.

How much someone selling his shares can expect to receive will depend on the demand for them, on the rate of interest and on the type of share. Some shares,

45 The new Royal Exchange in 1847. Addison, reflecting on an earlier Exchange, had said: 'There is no place in the town which I so much love to frequent as the Royal Exchange. It gives me a secret satisfaction, and in some measure gratifies my vanity, as I am an Englishman, to see so rich an assembly of countrymen and foreigners consulting together upon the private business of mankind, and making this metropolis a kind of emporium for the whole earth'

46 The Stock Exchange in Throgmorton Street in London

such as Preference Shares, receive interest before interest is paid on Ordinary Shares. Of course, if a particular company is doing badly it may not be paying dividends and so its shares can only be sold at a low price. Alternatively, if a company is riding high and paying high dividends, many people will want to buy its shares and the price of the shares rises accordingly.

The Stock Exchange publishes the prices of all securities quoted on the Stock Exchange. A holder of shares in any public company can easily look up just what his shares are worth at that time. Newspapers print the prices of some shares but, as there are about 10,000 securities quoted on the Stock Exchange, newspapers are only able to print a selection. A large part of the value of all this quoted stock (almost one half) is for Government securities.

If a company wants to expand or a new one wishes to raise money by issuing new shares to the public it must advertise, and set down its terms clearly. If the Government wants to borrow money from the public it also must publish an advertisement giving full details of the venture. This is called a prospectus.

71

Existing companies must report on their profits in the prospectus. New companies must estimate their expected profits.

If a company is being badly run, the Stock Exchange may exclude dealings in the shares of that company, either temporarily or permanently. So much depends on trust that the Stock Exchange is careful to see that quoted stock belongs to reliable companies only.

The Balance of Payments

Each person earns a certain amount of money in wages which he needs to pay for all the things he must buy in order to live. He cannot spend more than he earns without running into debt and trouble, and so he needs to balance his expenditure to match his income. In times of inflation, when prices rise fast, this can cause great problems and the wage-packet seems to disappear very quickly. Like a family or a business firm, the economy of the whole country must also be balanced so that we do not continually spend more than we have available. This is why the Government is always so concerned about the Balance of Payments. These accounts are a record of all transactions—of expenditure and of income—between people in Britain on the one hand and people throughout the rest of the world on the other. This statement of account is usually taken over a period of one year. However, the Balance of Payments of any country is a complex account, made up of many factors.

For example, it includes the Balance of Visible Trade, which is concerned with goods that are imported and exported. Britain imports many goods from all over the world and it is necessary to sell abroad as much as possible in order to pay for these imports. But, in fact, Britain usually imports far more goods than she exports and the difference is known as the Trade Gap. In 1956, 1958 and 1970, however, more goods were exported from Britain than were imported. In 1970 the value of 'visible' exports amounted to £7,885 millions and the value of goods imported totalled £7,882 millions.

Another account which forms part of the Balance of Payments is the Balance on Invisible Trade and such things as selling and paying for insurance, for holidays abroad, for journeys, for shipping services and numerous other services fall within this grouping. Britain and the United States of America each earn much money from 'invisible' world trade. So 'invisible' trade helps Britain to pay her way. The 'visible' and 'invisible' trade figures for 1970 are set down below in a simple table. Together they form the Balance of Payments on Current Account.

Current Account	*£ million*		
Visible Trade		Invisible Trade	
Exports	7,885	Receipts	4,860
Imports	7,882	Payments	4,284
Visible balance	+3	Invisible balance	+576

Current Balance of Payments = +579

But the situation is more complex than this because to work out a complete account of a country's financial transactions it is necessary to take into account capital imports and exports—loans, bank deposits and investments. 'Official' capital flows are amounts that the Government borrows or lends. 'Private' capital flows are borrowed or lent by companies or by individuals. There are still other flows of capital which must be taken into account in working out a country's total earning and spending, lending and borrowing. The position in 1970 can be set out as follows:

	£ million
Current Balance of Payments	+579
Investment and other Capital Flows	+615
Balancing item	+93
Total Currency Flow	+1287
Allocation of Special Drawing Rights	+171
Gold subscription to International Monetary Fund	−38
	+1420
Financed as follows:	
Official borrowing repaid	−1295
Additions to official reserves	−125
	−1420

If a country has a favourable Balance of Payments—and receipts of foreign currencies have exceeded payments made abroad—the credit balance helps to swell the country's savings of gold and supplies of foreign currency. But where the balance is unfavourable—and payments made abroad exceed receipts—the deficit is paid by taking money from reserves or by borrowing. Just how this is done is outlined in the next chapter.

Regulating the economy

The Government is able to exert a powerful influence on the economy in directions too numerous to discuss here. Domestic and foreign policies are each of joint importance. The health of the economy travels in waves. Sometimes conditions are unfavourable, people stop spending, demand for goods and services falls and the number of unemployed rises. 'Depressions' and 'slumps' affect the whole economy very quickly: in the 1930s only the pawn shop prospered in many parts of the country. The reverse happens when people continue to buy goods and services in quantity. Unemployment is much reduced and wages rise;

'boom' conditions result. But in conditions of inflation, when too much money is available to buy a limited quantity of goods, prices become very high.

In a depression, the Government does some of the spending that would normally be done by the public. Roads, schools and hospitals can be built and this gives work to the unemployed who can now start to spend again. Conversely, when people are spending too much the Government begins to 'squeeze' credit. Interest rates can be raised so that it costs more to borrow money. Taxes can be raised to make goods more expensive to buy and the banks are told not to lend money so readily. Wages can be frozen and so can profits as well as prices.

Prices in the internal market are of great importance in the international

47 Many people save their money in building societies and most of this money is lent to other people who want to buy their own homes. Investors are paid interest on the sum they save, and borrowers pay interest to the building society in addition to repaying the original sum they borrowed for their mortgage

trading scene too because, if prices and incomes rise greatly, the price of our export goods may become so high that they can no longer be sold competitively in countries overseas. If the prices of goods from abroad do not rise, they become cheaper for us to buy than goods produced in this country. In such a situation, without Government intervention to reduce consumer demand, the total Balance of Payments might become adversely affected to a very dangerous degree.

Further reading
G. Williams, *The Economics of Everyday Life* (Pelican)
P. Ferris, *The City* (Pelican)

7 International Money

Every country in the world has its own currency system. Most countries now work on the decimal system. The main unit of currency is divided into 100 parts. In Algeria 100 centimes equal one dinar, in Czechoslovakia 100 heller equal one crown and in Finland 100 pennis equal one markka. Other names for the main unit of currency in countries throughout the world include peseta, escudo, peso, dollar, pound, rand, lev, rupee, franc, krona, lira, yen, schilling, guilder, dirham, zloty, rouble, bolivar, sol—and many others. Some countries have the same name for their main unit of currency as used in other countries, though the value of these currencies is, of course, different in each country. For example, Denmark and Norway have krone, the USA, Antigua, Brunei, Canada, Fiji and Tonga all use dollars, and the United Kingdom, Egypt, Israel, Libya and Turkey all use the pound.

Money for travellers

When British tourists prepare to go abroad they must arrange to have money to spend when they get there. Someone going to the Netherlands for a fortnight on holiday must buy some Dutch money. British pounds are of little use in a foreign country and, in any case, there are restrictions on the amount of British money that a traveller may take abroad. Dutch money—like money of other countries—may be bought in several ways. A British branch bank will be able to obtain most foreign currencies for a traveller and usually a few days' notice is required. Another way for the traveller to obtain Dutch money is to wait until he arrives in the Netherlands and then buy it at a Dutch bank or exchange office. He can buy some foreign currency with the pound notes he is allowed to take abroad or he can change a traveller's cheque which he obtained at his own bank before he left home. A traveller's cheque is a piece of paper which looks very much like a bank note. Its advantage is that if it is stolen, lost or destroyed any local office abroad will refund the money promptly. If cash is lost or stolen, the traveller is in trouble, for unless he has made prior arrangements, he is unlikely to be given credit. Traveller's cheques are bought in various denominations and are kept in a wallet, which the bank provides, until the visitor wishes to cash one— they can be changed into any currency he needs. If someone is travelling through several different countries, and if he bought currency of each of these countries before leaving home, he may find that he has too much money left when he crosses the border into the next country, and these amounts must be constantly changed for other currencies at exchange offices. But if he holds traveller's cheques he can cash just the right amount that he needs into the local currency as his tour

48 The Stock Exchange at Zurich where bankers perform the function of stock brokers. Notice the sophisticated apparatus for assisting in buying and selling. Swiss financiers are often known as the 'gnomes of Zurich' because of their great influence on world-wide monetary business

progresses. When he returns home, any unused traveller's cheques are changed back into pounds by his bank. Traveller's cheques are a safe way of carrying money in Britain too and they can be changed at any bank and in many hotels.

A traveller in a foreign country must get used to the values of the currency in that country. In the Netherlands, for instance, 100 cents equal one guilder, and one guilder is worth about $11\frac{1}{2}$p in British money.

Most of us are only concerned about foreign money when we need some to use on holiday but other people spend their lives thinking about foreign money and working out the best ways of dealing with it. The banks, for example, supply foreign money to clients every day; someone somewhere always needs it for a foreign visit, and business firms are constantly seeking advice from the banks about how to pay for and receive payment for goods bought and sold abroad.

International trade

In the nineteenth century Britain became the most important trading country in the world. Much of the world's trade was financed through London and was quoted in pounds sterling. Foreign banks and companies abroad found that it was most convenient to settle debts in London and so they kept large amounts of sterling in British bank accounts where they could make payments and enter receipts. Even today, a quarter of all the world's trade is settled in pounds sterling because it is a respected and stable currency as its value does not often change greatly; also it is, like the dollar, a World Reserve Currency.

If an English manufacturer exports goods to the USA and is paid in dollars these cannot be used in England, and so he converts them into pounds. The banks are the main dealers in the London Foreign Exchange Market where all the main currencies of the world are bought and sold. Foreign exchange rates (for example, the exact amount in dollars that is obtained for a pound, and *vice versa*) vary frequently—usually by small amounts—and these changes depend on the supply of and the demand for the currencies at any time. If many people need to buy sterling to settle their debts in Britain, then the price of sterling will be high because it is so much in demand. Many exporters prefer to be paid in sterling or dollars when they sell goods to countries that have unstable monetary systems.

Suppose a company in Britain imports goods from a firm in Australia. The

49 Gold bars are being checked in the vaults of Johnson Matthey Bankers Ltd before despatch. Gold bars are very heavy, so people who move them must wear shoes which are specially reinforced in case of accidents. Hardly any countries now have gold coins for domestic use. The gold coins that are still minted —such as the British sovereign—are made for sale abroad and are bought by collectors. The main use of gold today is in jewellery. The Swiss Credit Bank in Zurich has a basement vault reached by a security lift and lined with metal shelves on which are large quantities of bullion and bars of palladium and platinum, worth many millions of pounds, and which are needed for daily business transactions. The bank's main storage vault is even further underground

British firm asks its bank to buy Australian dollars through the Foreign Exchange Market which it does at the rate of exchange current at that time. The amount due in Australian dollars is credited by the British bank to a bank in Australia with which it already does business. A letter, cable or telex is sent to the Australian bank authorising the relevant amount to be credited to the Australian firm of exporters. At the same time the British importer's account with the bank is debited in sterling with the cost of the imports.

The clearing banks have large foreign branches in London that deal only with international finance and, in addition, there are specialised branches in most important cities which deal with overseas trading. Even ordinary branch banks can advise on foreign trading. The foreign branches have teletype machines and direct lines to trading cities such as New York and Rome. Electronic calculators compute rates to as many as six decimal places.

Every country has its own central bank—the Bank of England in Britain, the Deutsche Bundesbank in Germany and the Federal Reserve System in the USA. Each central bank regulates the supply of the nation's money; its customers are the commercial banks, and it assists the Government in financial transactions. The Government in highly-developed countries is the main purchaser in the country and is constantly seeking advice about the best ways to make and receive payments.

50 The Chequemaster is a machine which allows cashiers to cash cheques for customers very quickly. The machine dispenses £1 and £5 notes as well as coins. The cashier records the amount the customer requests on an electronic keyboard. The Chequemaster prints details on the back of the cheque of the amount of cash paid out, and also dispenses the cash. It keeps a cumulative record of outgoings on a visual counter. The machine is being installed in banks that have a high rate of cashing cheques

51 Britain's largest cheque—£119,595,645 12s 0d—was written in 1961 for the take-over of the British Ford Motor Company. The largest cheque in the world was written in the USA in 1961 for over $960 million—more than £342 million

The International Monetary Fund

Before the First World War Britain had gold coins instead of pound notes. People all over the world accepted gold in payment because they knew they could rely on its value. The currency of every country was based on the value of gold. When countries were on the gold standard their currencies were fixed to a certain weight in gold and so these currencies were also linked to each other. If one currency was in great demand and its value rose, a point came when it was cheaper to transport gold and pay for goods in gold instead of buying expensive currency. But it was necessary for a country to try to get back gold when it lost some in this way and this interfered with the smooth working of the economy, resulting in periods of deflation and inflation.

In 1944 a conference was held at Bretton Woods in the USA to begin a new system of international trading that would help to increase world trade which had become much reduced during the Second World War and in the 1930s. An important aim was to devise means by which a country could be helped with temporary balance of payments problems. Two new institutions were evolved:

the International Bank and the International Monetary Fund. The International Bank aided reconstruction and development, and encouraged investment after the Second World War, as well as encouraging the growth of international trade. The International Monetary Fund (the IMF) is a sort of international central bank. Each member country contributed a proportion of its currency as well as some gold. Members can borrow from this fund when they need certain foreign currencies or gold in emergencies, but, of course, they cannot simply borrow again and again and there are restrictions and conditions. The difficulty is that whilst some currencies are frequently demanded, large parts of the total holdings of the IMF are hardly ever required.

The economist Lord Keynes suggested that a new monetary unit be devised to

52 A cashier at a television autobank talks to customers on the floor below through closed circuit television, and serves them by means of a pneumatic tube carrier

make international payments. He termed this unit *bancor*, which would have been a kind of world trading currency. This 'money' would have existed only as book entries at the IMF. National currencies would have been related to bancor instead of being related to gold.

It appears that the IMF does not have sufficient gold and foreign currencies to do its job effectively and some people think that the IMF should use paper claims to money—like cheques—and this system of 'Paper Gold' or Special Drawing Rights may dispense entirely with the need for gold to settle accounts. Others are more sceptical and even the Managing Director of the IMF has stated: 'Gold is a traditional means of international settlement and a point of reference for the values of national currencies. The value of Special Drawing Rights is guaranteed in terms of a weight of gold. More than one-half of all monetary reserves consists of gold, and it continues to be the basic element in the world monetary system.'

If a country with a persistent balance of payments problem has no foreign currency or gold to pay for imports it may decide on the extreme measure of devaluation, that is, of making its money cheaper abroad. Devaluation reduces the overseas value of a currency in terms of gold. This means that foreign currency becomes more expensive to buy. In 1967 the British pound was devalued by 14.3 per cent. As a result, foreign goods cost more to import into Britain and so imports were reduced, but, conversely, British goods then became cheaper to buy for countries abroad. The significance of devaluation is that it is hoped that lower export prices will result in more overseas sales, whilst the high prices of imports dampen sales of foreign goods in Britain. Of course, the expected increase in exports must be large enough to offset the lower price of each single good exported.

Further reading
P. Donaldson, *Guide to the British Economy* (Pelican)

8 The Decline of Cash

Speculations about the future of money are often harmless enough pastimes to indulge in. The difficulty is that we can never be absolutely sure what will actually happen in years to come. In the previous chapter the possibility of a single world currency was outlined. This present chapter goes to the other end of the spectrum and asks what appears to be the much more practical question: is cash important any longer? Is it simply out-of-date? Many people today manage to live perfectly well without always dipping into their pockets for cash. H.M. the Queen, who seldom handles money, has always managed this way. Members of the Royal Family very seldom carry cash. But, of course, like anyone else, what the Royal Family buys it must pay for. Accounts for goods that have

53 Members of the Royal Family sometimes visit shops, although the Queen seldom handles money. Here the Duchess of Kent takes Lord Nicholas into a sweet shop

been purchased are sent to the Court Treasurer and are settled by cheque. The Queen's bankers are Coutts and Co of London, and Royal cheques are signed by the secretary of the Privy Purse 'For and on behalf of Her Majesty's Privy Purse Department'.

The Queen's method of settling bills is different only in degree from that of very many British people today. Money is needed to pay for what we buy. But it is the *form* that the money takes which has tended to change over the last few decades. The number of people who have bank accounts has increased yearly.

At one time—not so long ago—most people who were paid weekly received a pay packet containing bank notes and coins. The traditional Friday—now often Thursday—evening on which this money was divided into different envelopes and purses to pay for the various items of household expenses still exists in many families. Everyone needs to budget. But a change has been happening in the method of paying wages and salaries. Millions of people, instead of receiving a pay packet, are now paid by cheque. Some of them receive this piece of paper at work at the end of the week or month. Others have their pay sent by the firm straight into a bank account of their choice. Such methods of paying wages save

54 Money museums trace the complex story of money forms from early times. In the Money Museum of the National Bank of Detroit the showcases are designed so that each side of the coins and other exhibits can be examined easily

55 The two parallel lines across this cheque show that it has been 'crossed'. Unlike an 'open' cheque, which can be cashed over the counter at the issuing bank, crossed cheques must be paid into a bank account. This is a security measure, since a lost or stolen crossed cheque that is paid into a bank account by a thief can always be traced. When writing the amount of money on a cheque, care should be taken to see that no spaces are left where additional words or figures could be inserted fraudulently. The banks supply cheques bound together as cheque books, and a cheque can be written and torn out when needed. Some cheque books are provided with counterfoils (as here, to the left of the cheque) on which the writer of the cheque records the details of his payment. Along the bottom of the cheque is the code line containing sets of figures. From left to right these are: the serial number of the cheque, the branch number of the bank and the customer's account number. The code numbers are printed in magnetic ink so that they can be 'read' automatically by electronic sorters

time and expense for the firm—which can then dispense with a large section of the clerks in its wages department—and from everyone's viewpoint such a method of payment is safer. It may be less convenient for the wage-earner who now has to go to his local bank to receive his pay; and the difficulty of getting to a bank during opening hours is a real problem for many people, unless the bank happens to be close by and they can pay a quick visit during their mid-day break.

When an employee goes to the bank for his money he can ask for the total amount due in notes and coins, or he can ask for part of this money only and leave the remainder in his account. Increasingly, the latter method is the one being adopted by very many people. Money can be left safely in a current bank account until it is needed to pay bills, and then a cheque can be written for any odd amount and sent through the post or delivered by hand. Writing cheques is quick, convenient and a lot safer and simpler than sending cash through the post or even carrying it around. The bank transfers the amount instructed on the cheque, the customer's account is debited by such an amount and the recipient's account is credited.

More and more people are finding that payment by cheque has advantages for making many kinds of payment. Instead of standing in a queue at the local council offices to pay your rate demand in bank notes and coin, it is easier to leave the

56 In 1743 a 500-ton treasure ship, the *Hollandia*, a Dutch East Indiaman, sank off the Scilly Isles with a large cargo of silver on board. It took three years of research and a further two years of diving before the wreck was located in 1971 by a diving team using an electronic detecting device. The wreck became the property of the divers and a percentage of the fortune they recovered went to the Dutch Government. All wrecks require careful excavation and the site of a find needs constant protection from pirate salvage teams. Within a few weeks of finding the *Hollandia* the divers had retrieved more than 3,000 silver Spanish pieces of eight and four, and Dutch ducatoons. Many of them bore the date 1742, the year before the ship was wrecked

money in your bank account and to write a cheque for the amount due, then post it to the treasurer at the council offices. Water rates, ground rent, telephone bills, bills from department stores, garages—and many others—can be paid in this way. As we saw in the chapter on banking, the work of banks is complex and manifold. Banks are much more than places to cash pay-cheques and to provide cheque books. One of the useful services banks provide for their customers is the standing order. You can instruct the bank to make a weekly, monthly or annual standing order for a certain amount to another individual or to a firm and the bank goes on doing this until you instruct them to stop. You might well forget that your insurance premium is due to be paid, that your annual subscription to a society or union is due or that your next mortgage repayment must be made. But banks do not forget. Money is their business, and they will debit your account of the relevant amount and credit the account of someone else. The system works well.

Increasingly, it is possible to pay one's bills and other commitments by not even seeing pound notes or coins. Money changes hands without either side holding cash. A computer transaction at the bank is the way that this is done.

The richer a person is, the less likely it is that he will handle coins and notes. He will write cheques and receive them—without ever touching cash. Cheques, of course, are not money. They are merely titles to bank money.

How far is it true, then, that money—in the sense of coins and bank notes—is obsolete and no longer needed? Certainly, many people manage without coins and bank notes for all except simple payments. The extended use of credit facilities has also resulted in people dispensing with such forms of money. Various forms of credit will be discussed later in this chapter. They all allow people to enjoy goods whilst they are paying for them—often not even a deposit is required for many kinds of purchases—and so buyers enjoy the delay of eventual repayment in full. Often repayments are made by cheque or by standing order and so here, as in other fields, cash payments are often rendered obsolete.

The value of bank deposits is now much greater than the amount of coins and notes in circulation. The growth of modern banking has resulted in bank money becoming increasingly important. Bank notes and coins are now the 'small change' of the economic system. Bank money exceeds by several times the amount of notes and coins in existence.

The amount of coins that the Royal Mint produces and the number of bank notes which are printed by the Bank of England depend on the demand of the public to hold its money in that form—instead of as bank money. The public needs increased supplies of pound notes and coins during holiday periods and during the Christmas shopping spree. The Royal Mint and the Bank of England's printing works at Debden in Essex must be ready to meet this temporarily increased demand.

At one time cash was something of a status symbol. The man with a walletful of 'fivers' was looked to with respect. Times are changing, however, and he is now more likely to carry a cheque book. Some firms even tend to be suspicious of customers who want to settle their bills with large sums of cash. Can they not be trusted with a cheque book or credit card?

Some experts say that by the end of the twentieth century Britain should be in a position to manage without any coins or bank notes. But it seems unlikely that this situation will ever be reached. It is quite possible at present to live without ever handling cash, but very few people do so. Cash will always be needed for small purchases in shops where customers are not known. Emergencies occur, and taxi, bus and train fares are paid in cash. Then there are the machines—for sweets, cigarettes, stamps, telephone boxes, parking meters—which take coins. In business, as in government and industry, cash plays a minor—even an insignificant—role. But the average individual needs his small change for the ordinary business of small daily purchases. Probably British money habits will undergo even further changes away from holding pocketfuls of cash. Inflation will help to hasten this change. Every year money buys less and less for every pound. What can be bought with coins shrinks almost monthly. As this trend continues, our coinage especially will be shown to be unsatisfactory and even pointless. Small coins such as the farthing, the half-penny and the threepence have disappeared in recent history. Perhaps the time will not be long in coming for other coins to follow along the same path.

In early times men used countless articles as money. Provided that they were accepted as such by all who traded together, it mattered little what those articles might be. In the last analysis the article itself is of relative unimportance. Money is only a means towards an end. What it will buy in exchange is the all-important factor. It seems a far cry from cowrie shells and cattle as articles of exchange to pound notes and tenpence pieces. But though bank notes and coinage have served us well for so many centuries we must not be led into a false feeling that they are the final answer in the evolution of money forms. The evolution of banking in our own age should warn us against such illusions of permanence. Bank money is now the predominant form in which money is held in Britain. In this sense, coins and bank notes are indeed dated forms of money. Probably it will be many years—if ever—before any economy dispenses entirely with cash as we now know it; but the mere fact that individuals within any advanced economy are able to do so if they choose shows us that forms of money as instruments of exchange are still evolving.

Buying on credit

The United States of America has carried the change to bank money further than anywhere else. Though cash is still used universally in that country, credit cards are used everywhere. Hotels, shops, restaurants, air-lines, garages and supermarkets all accept credit cards and at least one church in San Francisco has a sign outside stating that credit cards are accepted instead of coins on the collection plate!

Credit cards and other forms of 'have now, pay later' have become of such importance in the United States, in Britain and in other developed countries that it is essential for us to take a closer look at these various kinds of credit, for

57 The credit card is a convenient way to pay for goods and services at a later date. Many garages, hotels, restaurants and shops have already joined the scheme. Credit cards can also be used in many countries abroad. Holders of credit cards enjoy the immediate use of goods and services and also the advantage of extended credit for almost a month before payment is due

58 A computer does four main jobs in working out a bank's book-keeping: it receives information, stores it, processes it and provides the answers to calculations. Detailed instructions must be written and implemented by specialists, known as systems analysts and programmers, so that the computer knows how to deal with information. These instructions are called programmes and are in the form of a great many logical operations set out in the particular 'language' to which the computer is accustomed. This picture shows a large computer room. A computer operator is seated at the special typewriter which is connected directly to the computer

they affect every one of us, and some of us to a very great degree. There was a time in the past when many people frowned on those who obtained goods before they could afford to pay for them completely. There are still those who prefer to pay 'cash on the nail' but times have changed and now even the best and promptest payers cannot avoid living partly on credit. Most of us enjoy newspapers, milk, gas, electricity and telephones and then, after a period, we receive a bill for the amount we have used.

Many people buy important items of furniture and cars on hire purchase. Sometimes a deposit must be paid and then instalments at regular intervals until the item is paid for in full. Of course, paying in this way costs the purchaser more than it does if he pays the original lump sum all at once, but so many items can be bought in this way—even holidays under 'go now, pay later' schemes— that hire purchase has become an important part of modern living.

Houses are bought under a similar scheme. The buyer sends a mortgage repayment monthly to a building society, every payment incorporating interest and also repayment on the capital sum lent to the house-buyer.

Buying articles under credit sales, the purchaser owns the articles from the

59 This picture shows the computer room of the Clearing Department of Barclays Bank in London. Information can be transferred to magnetic tape, discs, punched paper tape or punched cards and stored there. This information is represented by varying patterns of magnetised spots on tape and on discs (an idea rather similar to that used in the tape recorder and the record player), and by coded information in holes punched in various positions on punched cards and on punched tape. Information can be fed into the computer. The computer operator then instructs the computer to do a certain job and the answer obtained can be stored for later use, in any of the forms already mentioned; or it can be printed out on large sheets of paper for immediate use. A recent development is the linking of a branch bank directly to the computer centre via post office telephone lines. Entries can be sent to the computer to be added to customers' accounts and the branch can receive information typed out on a keyboard. A branch bank can ask the computer questions about any customer's account and receive an answer almost immediately

start. Such articles are not 'on hire'. Five per cent interest is often added to the cash price by the shop, and the bill may be settled in monthly instalments.

Overdrafts and loans

When a bank gives a customer an overdraft, it allows him to write cheques for a sum in excess of the amount of money in his account. Interest is charged on the overdrawn balance. Usually the customer must offer the bank some security to show that he has something in hand which the bank could turn into cash should he default in his repayments, such as the deeds to a house or a life assurance policy.

Banks also offer personal loans to customers. These are usually repaid at monthly intervals and a credit charge is added to the original sum. The terms and period of a personal loan are fixed, unlike the overdraft which in theory can be called in by the bank without notice. To obtain a personal loan a customer may need to offer the bank, as security, proof that he has a regular income.

Special facilities for shoppers

Large department stores provide budget accounts for customers. A fixed sum is paid to the store each month and credit may be offered to about eight times the monthly payment. Often regular customers also have monthly accounts at large stores. They buy what they choose and merely sign for it and at the end of the month they receive a bill for all they have bought and they pay the bill in cash or with one cheque. Credit is thus given for one month without extra charge provided the account is paid promptly when it falls due.

Many shoppers make use of trading cheque facilities. These can be either bought from the organisations that issue them or they can be written when they are needed for exact amounts. A trading cheque for £10 perhaps costs about £10.50 to pay back, probably at 50p a week for 21 weeks. In either case, a representative calls at the buyer's home to collect the amount due each week. A disadvantage is that trading cheques can only be spent at shops displaying the trader's sign.

Many housewives, and especially those who find shopping difficult, enjoy buying goods without leaving their home by joining a home shopping club. Members receive a copy of the coloured catalogue which lists all the goods which the club offers for sale. Goods ordered are paid for by instalments.

Of course cheques issued by banks, as we have seen already, move money from one bank account to another and the signing of a cheque gives credit at least for a time, until the person to whom the cheque is paid passes it through the bank.

Credit clearing

Credit clearing in the banking system operates in a similar way to the general clearing of cheques. Credit clearing is part of the Bank Giro system. A credit transfer enables payments to be made direct into a customer's account at any bank. This dispenses with the need to buy postal orders or money orders or to send cheques through the post. Every year about two hundred million credit vouchers pass through credit clearing and through the Inter-Bank Computer Bureau, the latter of which is a computerised clearing house. Most standing orders, for instance, are passed through the Bureau on magnetic tape and in time this system will help towards even greater economy as the number of paper vouchers needed will be greatly reduced.

Cheque and credit cards

Cheque cards are another form of credit which are issued by banks on request to customers whom they can trust. The customer must sign his cheque card and then the bank guarantees payment of that person's cheques to a stated amount. If someone with a cheque book is travelling in a strange town and wishes to give a cheque to a trader the latter might wonder whether the cheque will be honoured. Anyone with a cheque book can write a cheque for £1,000 whether he has that much money in his bank account or not. But if the money in his account cannot

60 A Victorian post office about 1860, showing customers rushing to post letters and newspapers before the post office closed for the night

cover a large cheque then the cheque is said to 'bounce' as the bank returns it to the trader, and then legal trouble might start. Of course, often traders are prepared to accept cheques without question, but for large amounts—and especially if the cheque book owner is unknown to the trader—the possession of a cheque card guarantees the trader payment when he passes the cheque through the banking system.

Credit cards are also issued by banks and they allow the holder to buy goods or services at shops, restaurants, garages—or anywhere else which belongs to the credit card scheme. The buyer does not pay cash or present a cheque when he makes his purchases. He merely shows his credit card and signs the bill. The firm from which he has bought goods then sends a copy of the bill to the bank that issued the credit card. The bank settles the bill with the firm at once. The purchaser retains his copy of the bill and at the end of the month his bank sends him a statement which shows all the transactions he has made with his credit card during that month. He settles this amount by making one payment to his bank— usually by writing a cheque. Very many firms now accept credit cards and many people buy a considerable part of their purchases in this way. Of course, a credit card must be used with care or a wreckless purchaser could find it easy to

61 The modern post office at the Stock Exchange in London, with anti-bandit screens. There are 1,700 post offices in Britain and 23,000 sub-offices. The National Savings Bank is conducted through post offices, which are also used by the Government to distribute money—from family allowances to old age pensions—all over the country

overspend and trouble would result at the end of the month. In fact, when customers are issued with credit cards the bank informs them of their credit limit, which is the maximum amount of money they are allowed to have outstanding. A credit card allows a customer to cash a cheque up to his credit limit in any branch belonging to the bank that issued it.

Each of these methods of delaying payment and of making payment without the direct use of cash takes us some little distance along the road towards a cashless society.

Further reading
R. Hendrickson, *The Future of Money* (MacGibbon & Kee)
E. Bullard, *The Language of Machines* (I.B.M.)

Glossary

angel	an old gold coin
assay	to test the proportion of metal in a coin
bimetallic	both gold and silver used as currency to any amount
bond	an official promise to repay borrowed money
broker	a dealer who buys and sells for clients
cheque	an order to a bank to pay money to a certain person, or to the bearer
consumer demand	the effective buying power of the population
convertible currency	money that could be exchanged for gold or silver (up to 1931 in Britain)
counterfeiting	making illegal imitation copies
credit	money or goods provided to be paid for at a later date
crown	a coin of five shillings (25p)
debase	to lower the quantity of valuable metal in coins
dividend	profits distributed to shareholders
farthing	one quarter of an old penny
florin	one tenth of a pound (10p)
gold reserve	stocks of gold held by the central bank
gold standard	the situation when currency is worth a fixed amount of gold, and banknotes may be exchanged for the gold at which they are valued
Government stock	certificates representing a loan to the Government bearing fixed interest—sometimes called gilt-edged stock
groat	an old fourpence coin
guinea	a gold coin valued at one pound, one shilling (£1.05)
ingot	a bar of metal
insolvent	inability to repay what is owed
interest	profit obtained from lending money for a period
jobber	a specialist in buying and selling stock of a particular kind on stock exchanges
joint stock	a form of business which is owned by shareholders
legal tender	the value up to which coins (limited amount) and banknotes must be legally accepted in payment
money market	a market in bills for short-period loans
numismatic	pertaining to coins
obverse	the 'front' of a coin, bearing the monarch's head
penny (d)	one-twelfth of a shilling

profits	the money gained from a venture
reverse	the 'back' of a coin
ryal	a gold coin
securities	certificates of a loan, stock, bond etc
shareholder	someone who owns shares in a company, and so a part-owner
shilling	one-twentieth of a pound (5p)
sovereign	a gold coin worth £1
the Treasury	the Government department which manages the finances of the country
Treasury bills	bills issued by the Government to raise money for short-term needs
unbacked notes	banknotes not covered by stocks of gold
votive	religious offering
watermark	a pattern incorporated in the paper during manufacture
World Reserve Currency	a currency (such as sterling or dollars) which is used throughout the world as an international currency

Index

Numbers in **bold type** refer to the figure numbers of the illustrations.